DUALISM AND POLARITY
IN THE NOVELS OF RAMÓN PÉREZ DE AYALA

MARGARET POL STOCK

DUALISM AND POLARITY IN THE NOVELS OF RAMÓN PÉREZ DE AYALA

TAMESIS BOOKS LIMITED
LONDON

Colección Támesis
SERIE A - MONOGRAFIAS, CXXVII

DISTRIBUTORS:

Spain:
Editorial Castalia,
Zurbano, 39,
28010 Madrid

United States and Canada:
Longwood Publishing Group,
27 South Main Street,
Wolfeboro, New Hampshire 03894-2069, U.S.A.

Great Britain and rest of the world:
Grant and Cutler Ltd.,
55-57 Great Marlborough Street,
London W1V 2AY

ISBN.: 84-599-2247-2
Depósito Legal: M-2072-1988.
Printed in Spain by Unigraf, S.A. Móstoles, Madrid.

for
TAMESIS BOOKS LIMITED
LONDON

TABLE OF CONTENTS

PREFACE

To my mentors, Dr and Mrs Dean W. McPheeters and Dr and Mrs William J. Smither, with appreciation for their editing and advice. I also wish to express my appreciation to the University of South Alabama for its collaboration and support.

MARGARET POL STOCK

University of South Alabama
Mobile, Alabama, U.S.A.

FOREWORD

An important theme in the literature of the last hundred years has been the problem of the *Doppelgänger* or double. The divided personality of twentieth-century man and his quest for integration of the self have preoccupied such authors as Unamuno, Cortázar and Carlos Fuentes, among others. The double is a natural result of Plato's division into the ideal and the real, a concept later reinforced by the Christian religion and which became basic to the Western psyche.

Many critics have noted Ramón Pérez de Ayala's fondness for contrasts and paired opposites. His Jesuit training and education in the classics of both Greece and Spain helped form the author's dualistic frame of mind. However, his novels exhibit a progression from clear-cut dualisms in the early tetralogy to a more polaristic view in his middle novels and, finally, to integration in the person of Tigre Juan, the protagonist of his last novel.

While Pérez de Ayala's first novels are replete with paired opposites, later the oppositions are between such major themes as the dualisms of spectator and actor, *voluntad* and *abulia,* the ideal and the real, and, finally, the most basic dualism of all—the male and the female. Similarly, whereas the characters of the early novels are extreme examples of one dualism or another, in the later novels they become polaristic. The best example of this evolution is the meshing of the personalities of Belarmino and Apolonio. In a like manner, Urbano is able to change from *abulia* to *voluntad,* thus showing that the two are not irreconcilable opposites but, instead, poles that can be interchanged depending on the circumstances. In the two volumes dedicated to Tigre Juan, which together comprise Pérez de Ayala's last novel, the dualisms have been integrated; the protagonist is a harmonious blend of spectator and actor and the dualism of *voluntad* and *abulia* has disappeared. Moreover, by discarding the persona and confronting the self, Tigre Juan is able to integrate the dualism of the ideal versus the real by humanizing the Don Juan and *honra* traditions of Spanish culture.

Starting with *Belarmino y Apolonio,* there is a growing number of personages that combine contradictory traits and, in particular, increasing use of the androgynous character. Again Tigre Juan serves as a hermaph-

11

roditic whole. Appropriately, *El curandero de su honra* concludes with Tigre Juan's song praising the harmony of the universe.

This book ended Pérez de Ayala's novelistic career; afterwards he wrote only essays and poetry. The journey toward self-discovery which had started in his autobiographical tetralogy ended with the Tigre Juan novels. Through this progression, Pérez de Ayala had solved for himself the problem of the *Doppelgänger*.

1

PÉREZ DE AYALA'S SEARCH FOR UNITY

Ramón Pérez de Ayala, novelist, poet, and essayist, can be considered the last of Spain's celebrated Generation of '98. The youngest member of that group, born in 1880, he wrote his most important novels in the 1920s. The last novels, *Belarmino y Apolonio* (1921), *Luna de miel, luna de hiel / Los trabajos de Urbano y Simona* (1923), and *Tigre Juan / El curandero de su honra* (1926) show most clearly Pérez de Ayala's preoccupation with dualism and polarity, as the very titles indicate. However, dualistic elements can be found in all his novels, even in the early ones.

In this study, I make the distinction between dualism and polarity proposed by Alan W. Watts:

> What, exactly, is polarity? It is something much more than simple duality or opposition. For to say that opposites are *polar* is to say much more than that they are far apart: it is to say that they are related and joined—that they are the terms, ends, or extremities of a single whole. Polar opposites are therefore *inseparable* opposites, like the poles of the earth or of a magnet, or the ends of a stick or the faces of a coin. [1]

We conceive of dualism as two lines that run parallel to each other; they need each other to be parallel, but they can never be united. Polarity, on the other hand, is composed of opposites that have an integrating axis and are thus related and joined.

Watts then goes on to explain that Christianity is essentially dualistic and makes a clear distinction between God and the Devil, good and evil, the spirit and the body, whereas Eastern religions are polaristic and emphasize that all opposites are poles of one whole (the yin/yang principle).

From his earliest novels and in his poetry, Pérez de Ayala deals with duality and polarity, and his works display an intense desire for integration

---

[1] ALAN W. WATTS, *The Two Hands of God. The Myths of Polarity* (New York: George Braziller, 1963), p. 49.

13

and unity. This desire for integration shows a progression throughout his works and he seems to have achieved it in his last novels.

There are many possible explanations for Pérez de Ayala's interest in dualism and polarity. First of all, duality has a long tradition in Spanish letters; it can be seen in *El gran teatro del mundo* by Calderón and, of course, in the famous pair, Don Quijote and Sancho Panza. In fact, Unamuno in his chapter on «disociación» in *En torno al casticismo* seems to consider duality an integral part of the Spanish psyche. But Unamuno, like Pérez de Ayala, rebels against this duality, this separation between mind and body. Unamuno criticizes the mystics like Santa Teresa or San Juan de la Cruz who achieve the mystical experience by retreating inside themselves and leaving the world behind. He admires more the humanistic mysticism of Fray Luis de León who, by looking outside himself at nature, is able to join heaven and earth.

In their desire to integrate opposites, Unamuno and Pérez de Ayala seem to have understood each other. A sample of their correspondence, a letter that Ayala wrote to Unamuno in 1912, bears out this supposition:

> Bueno; vaya por anticipado que para mí, ridículo cómico y tragedia individual son términos equivalentes. ... De suerte que estoy conforme con Vd. Y cuando Vd. dice que Vd. es un humorista feroz, este adjetivo me parece un acierto, y entiendo que encierra esas dos ideas, la de ver el ridículo cómico —humor— y comprender que en la conciencia del individuo es una tragedia —ferocidad. [2]

As is well known, Unamuno rebelled against the dictatorship of rationalism. In fact, the whole twentieth century and a great part of the nineteenth, starting with the Romantics, might be viewed as an attempt by man to shake off the bonds of reason and give supremacy to feelings. Nietzsche's idea of the will to power and of the superman did away with conventional morality's concepts of good and evil and led the way to a more perspectivistic view of reality, as explained by Ortega y Gasset:

> Es inconcebible la dificultad que encuentran algunas gentes para aceptar la inevitable duplicidad que, a menudo, lo real nos presenta. Ello es que sólo quieren quedarse con un haz de las cosas y niegan o enturbian el otro haz contradictorio. Etica y jurídicamente, podrá ser Napoleón un forajido ... pero, quiérase o no, es evidente que en él dio la estructura humana altísimas pulsaciones... [3]

Freud's work on dreams showed the power of the irrational forces in man and how they guide his conscious actions without his even knowing it, and, in 1905, Einstein's theory of relativity, in which he proved

---

[2] ANDRÉS AMORÓS, *La novela intelectual de Ramón Pérez de Ayala* (Madrid: Editorial Gredos, 1972), p. 466.
[3] JOSÉ ORTEGA Y GASSET, *El tema de nuestro tiempo* (Madrid: Calpe, 1923), p. 126.

that dimensions were not absolutes after all, but that their measurements depended on the point of reference from which these measurements were taken, did away with the concept of any and all absolutes in the universe.[4] Man now realized that Truth was a matter of perspective. Some, like the cubists, tried to integrate the various perspectives by presenting an object from all its points of view at once. Others, like Ortega, decided that man was incapable of integrating all perspectives into one whole but that Truth was a summary of the various perspectives: «Cada individuo es un punto de vista esencial. Yuxtaponiendo las visiones parciales de todos se lograría tejer la verdad omnímoda y absoluta.»[5]

In fact, Ortega y Gasset devoted a whole book, *El tema de nuestro tiempo,* to the subject of perspectivism. In his study of reason as the cause of the dualism inherent in occidental culture, he claims that as soon as Socrates discovered reason, Europe, as separate from Asia, was born:

> Porque no debe olvidarse que la cultura, la razón, no han existido desde siempre en la tierra. Hubo un momento... en que se descubre el polo objetivo de la vida: la razón. Puede decirse que en ese día nace Europa como tal. Hasta entonces, la existencia en nuestro continente se confundía con la que había sido en Asia o en Egipto. Pero un día, en las plazuelas de Atenas, Sócrates descubre la razón...[6]

Then Ortega goes on to say that this rationalism causes a dualism, a double life, in which pure reason, the non-spontaneous, becomes more important than what we really are, the spontaneous life force.[7] Reason, he says, needs to categorize, but categorizing divides and separates:

> Por muy impenetrables que dos cuerpos sean, lo son mucho más dos conceptos. La Identidad, por ejemplo, ofrece una absoluta resistencia a confundirse con la Diferencia. El hombre virtuoso es siempre, a la vez, más o menos vicioso; pero la Virtud está exenta de Vicio. Los conceptos puros son, pues, más claros, más inequívocos ... que las cosas de nuestro contorno vital...[8]

Reason, and the culture that it engenders is «antivital», a concept shared by Unamuno but solved by resorting to the absurd and the irrational, whereas Ortega elaborates a metaphysical stance which he calls «la razón vital»:

> No se habría llegado a tal disociación ... si junto al imperativo de objetividad se nos hubiese predicado el de lealtad con nosotros mismos, que resume

---

[4] Pérez de Ayala and Einstein were good friends, so much so that the physicist lodged at the author's home in London. During these visits, the two would converse and exchange ideas late into the night. See EDUARDO PÉREZ DE AYALA Y RICK, «D. Ramón Pérez de Ayala visto por su hijo Eduardo», in *Pérez de Ayala en su centenario, 1880-1980* (Oviedo: Instituto de Estudios Asturianos, 1981), pp. 145-46.

[5] ORTEGA Y GASSET, p. 157.

[6] ORTEGA Y GASSET, p. 86.

[7] ORTEGA Y GASSET, p. 90.

[8] ORTEGA Y GASSET, p. 88.

la serie de los imperativos vitales. Es menester que en todo momento estemos en claro sobre si, en efecto, creemos lo que presumimos creer; si, en efecto, el ideal ético que «oficialmente» aceptamos, interesa e incita las energías profundas de nuestra personalidad. Con esta continua «mise au point» de nuestra situación íntima, habríamos ejecutado automáticamente una selección en la cultura, y hubiéranse eliminado todas aquellas formas de ella que son incompatibles con la vida, que son utópicas y conducen a la hipocresía. [9]

Ortega also points out in *El tema de nuestro tiempo* that this dichotomy between reason and life does not exist in oriental cultures. [10] The similarities between Ortega y Gasset and Pérez de Ayala in their views on perspectivism have been well-studied by Mariano Baquero Goyanes and by Frances Wyers Weber. I would like to suggest, however, that in addition to sharing views on perspectivism, Ortega and Pérez de Ayala also shared a knowledge of and appreciation for the unity of spirit and matter that is the basis of oriental philosophies.

Most critics have tended to ignore the influence of orientalism on the writers of the late nineteenth and early twentieth centuries. Edward W. Said, in his book *Orientalism,* has studied its influence on English and French authors, but largely in terms of the imperialistic goals of France and England in the Middle East, rather than the influence that oriental philosophies might have had on the writers. But it is a well-known fact that many of the «rebel» poets of the nineteenth century, such as Baudelaire in France and the Modernists in Latin America, were well acquainted with oriental philosophies and fascinated by the occult. Orientalism was in fashion among the intellectuals, and Pérez de Ayala's friendship with Ramón del Valle-Inclán and Enrique Gómez Carrillo leads us to believe that he was familiar with oriental thought. [11] Octavio Paz is the only critic who mentions the influence of the occult on modern writers but points out that «nuestra crítica apenas si se detiene en ella, como si se tratase de algo vergonzoso». [12]

Some of the salient points of oriental philosophies are evident, in my belief, in the works of Pérez de Ayala. First, his fascination with myths is obvious. In this regard, Watts says:

To the extent that myth is primitive philosophy, such philosophy would have a sharper intuition of the world's ambivalence than the either/or style of more logical thinking. There are numerous folk tales having to do with the fundamental partnership of God and the Devil. [13]

[9] ORTEGA Y GASSET, pp. 78-79.
[10] ORTEGA Y GASSET, p. 83.
[11] Valle-Inclán and Gómez Carrillo both appear in *Troteras y danzaderas* under the pseudonyms of Monte Valdés and Trelles, «el guatemalteco», respectively.
[12] OCTAVIO PAZ, *Los hijos del limo. Del romanticismo a la vanguardia* (Barcelona: Editorial Seix Barral, 1974), p. 133.
[13] WATTS, p. 29.

Pérez de Ayala dealt only with Western myths. Nevertheless, I think the analogy can be made and the conclusion reached that all myths are essentially polaristic. In Christianity there seems to be an unbridgeable gulf between Good and Evil, whereas in oriental philosophies Good and Evil need each other and are integrated into one whole, the yin/yang principle. This principle integrates not only Good and Evil but all opposites:

> These terms are said to have been first applied to the south and north sides of mountains, the former sunny and the latter shady. As the two sides of a mountain are an inseparable polarity, *yang* and *yin* came to signify the archetypal poles of nature—plus and minus, strong and yielding, man and woman, light and darkness, rising and falling. [14]

«The successive movement of *yin* and *yang*», Watts then says, «constitutes what is called the Way (Tao)». [15] (It is notable that Pérez de Ayala called his books of poetry *senderos*.)

> A clear and complete perception of the implicit unity of the *yang* and *yin* principles ... would include the realization of the same unity between the self and the not-self, the world inside the skin and the world outside. [16]

In his last novels, Pérez de Ayala makes a conscious and, in the view of some critics, a somewhat forced attempt to reconcile antagonistic selves, notably Belarmino with Apolonio and Tigre Juan with Vespasiano.

One need not look as far as the Orient to find attempts at integration of dualism and polarity. Pérez de Ayala was well-versed in the classics; indeed, in the opinion of Andrés Amorós, Pérez de Ayala's concern with harmony and balance is a result of his classical education. In this regard, Watts mentions one of Heraclitus's aphorisms: «Opposition brings concord. Out of discord comes the fairest harmony», [17] but it should also be pointed out that Heraclitus antedated Socrates, and, in the opinion of Ortega, Socrates and reason separated West from East. Thus Heraclitus would still be thinking as an Oriental. Julio Cejador y Frauca finds the Greek and Roman classicism of Pérez de Ayala to be «alumbrado por el espíritu español de nuestros humanistas», [18] and Amorós also mentions a Petrarchist influence, as a result of which Ayala sees the world «como guerra y coexistencia de contrastes». [19]

Humanism led to rationalism, and rationalism, for three hundred years in Europe, was Descartes. However, another rationalist, Baruch Spinoza,

---

[14] WATTS, p. 54.
[15] WATTS, p. 57.
[16] WATTS, p. 68.
[17] WATTS, p. 51.
[18] JULIO CEJADOR Y FRAUCA, «Don Ramón Pérez de Ayala», in *De la tierra* (Madrid: Jubera Hnos., 1914), p. 246.
[19] AMORÓS, *La novela intelectual*, p. 28.

although he considered himself a disciple of Descartes, came to have quite a different view of life. Pérez de Ayala is fond of the expression *sub specie aeterni,* which stands for «universal substantive whole» and is the basis for Spinoza's philosophy. [20] In Spinoza, we already have perspectivism:

> Suppose, he said in a letter, that a parasitic worm living in the bloodstream tried to make sense of its surroundings: from the point of view of the worm, each drop of blood would appear as an independent whole and not as a part of a total system. The worm would not recognize that each drop behaves as it does in virtue of the nature of the bloodstream as a whole. ... If we men begin with the bodies that surround us in nature and treat them as independent wholes..., then we shall be in error precisely as the worm is in error. We must grasp the system as a whole before we can hope to grasp the nature of the part, since the nature of the part is determined by its role in the total system. ... The whole is a single system which has two names, «God» and «Nature». [21]

Since God and Nature are the same, they are inseparable and therefore the duality that is at the heart of our Judeo-Christian tradition is obliterated. Moreover:

> God is understood to be the immanent and continuing cause of the world and not its transient first cause. He thus rejects the view ... that God is the first, efficient, external cause of the world's being and motion but that thereafter the world continues according to divinely ordained mechanical laws. The scientist looks and need look only as far as those laws; the theologian looks beyond, to the lawmaker. This deistic compromise allows science and theology their own territories; Spinoza's doctrine of the one substance insists upon a unitary doctrine in which every issue between them must be resolved. [22]

Another duality which Spinoza attacks is that of the body and mind. For Descartes, the senses are to be mistrusted; the only affirmation of reality is what the mind can establish through reason. But for Spinoza, body and mind

> are identical, because thought and extension are two attributes under which the one substance is conceived. Spinoza's doctrine of substance and attributes is not merely an assertion of the unity of the single substance but an attempt to explain the relationship between that unity and the multiplicity of finite beings. [23]

There are several similarities between Spinoza and Tao philosophy which seem appropriate to a discussion of Pérez de Ayala's search for

---

[20] Telephone conversation with Dr Robert C. Whittemore, Professor of Philosophy, Tulane University, 26 April 1983.
[21] *The Encyclopedia of Philosophy,* 1967 ed., s.v. «Spinoza, Benedict (Baruch)», by ALASDAIR MACINTYRE, p. 531.
[22] *The Encyclopedia of Philosophy,* p. 533.
[23] *The Encyclopedia of Philosophy,* p. 534.

unity. In the first place, it is interesting here to compare Spinoza's concept of God as continuous motion with the yin/yang principle which is also a continuously moving force. In addition, Tao, like Spinoza, is essentially monistic:

> Thus to become a *hsien* was, at root, to take conscious possession of one's true and original body—the world, and this by quite literally coming to one's senses, which, after all, do the work of integration for us. Light, color, shape, weight, and texture are all states of a nervous system and a body which, in its turn, is an integral part of the rainbow-world seen in these terms. But man cuts himself off from it and loses the sense of his original body by considering himself as an «I» which has these experiences, standing back from them just as one looks at a picture. [24]

Descartes and Spinoza also differ in their views on truth and error. For Descartes, error is the result of man's will rejecting what his reason dictates. On the other hand,

> Spinoza avoids any suggestion of this by an account of truth which allows for error and falsity from the outset. Since error and falsity are a privation of truth, in recognizing what is true, we also gradually come to recognize what is false. [25]

For various reasons it may be difficult to pinpoint influences on Pérez de Ayala. He was extremely well-read in several languages and may have picked up influences from a variety of sources. Andrés Amorós emphasizes Pérez de Ayala's classical education; Julio Cejador points out his acquaintance with the humanistic classics of Spanish literature; Frances Weber seems to have based her book primarily on Ortega's views on perspectivism, perhaps influenced in this by Baquero Goyanes; and I have suggested that there might be influences from the oriental philosophies and Spinoza.

Baquero Goyanes has shown Ayala's penchant for contrast and his use of perspectivism, but the critic who deals most thoroughly with the problem of dualism and perspectivism in Pérez de Ayala is Frances Weber. However, her work focuses mostly on perspectivism from several angles: that of the narrator, that of the characters, from the point of view of language and then from that of reality versus art. Her study emphasizes the multi-faceted aspects of perspectivism.

Obviously perspectivism is an important aspect of Pérez de Ayala's work. Nevertheless, it seems that the basic concept that concerns the author is the duality and polarity of the universe, and he uses perspectivism primarily to emphasize their analogy. For example, the novel *Belarmino*

---

[24] WATTS, p. 70.
[25] *Encyclopedia of Philosophy*, «Spinoza», p. 538.

y Apolonio may have much perspectivism, but the main idea of the novel is the polarity between the two protagonists/antagonists. Weber mentions that «he may present the antagonists in a novel as the severed halves of a single unit, each complementing and fulfilling the other...», [26] but she does not elaborate on this polar theme.

I propose to study specifically duality and polarity in the novels of Pérez de Ayala. Naturally, I shall mention his use of perspectivism, but only as it regards his attempts to integrate duality. His early tetralogy is essentially dualistic and this dualism causes anguish for the protagonist, Alberto Díaz de Guzmán. However, by the time he wrote his last novels, Pérez de Ayala was able to reconcile these opposites. In other words, he shifted from a dualistic to a polaristic view of the world. It is possible that this shift took place during the period in which he was writing his *Tres novelas poemáticas de la vida española* (1916). In 1913 Pérez de Ayala married, and in 1914 his first son was born. Perhaps marriage and fatherhood matured him and made him more tolerant, which might account for the duality of his early works in contrast to the polarity and loving acceptance of his later novels.

---

[26] FRANCES WYERS WEBER, *The Literary Perspectivism of Ramón Pérez de Ayala* (Chapel Hill: The University of North Carolina Press, 1966), p. 46.

THE TETRALOGY OF ALBERTO DÍAZ DE GUZMÁN

Pérez de Ayala's first novel, *Tinieblas en las cumbres,* appeared in 1907 under the pseudonym of Plotino Cuevas. Starting with the first page, the author presents one of those contrasting pairs that he will use again and again throughout the tetralogy and in his later novels: «Las descripciones de Cerda y Jiménez... contrastan en el buen aspecto exterior y tendencia a la lujuria y concupiscencia del uno, y el mal aspecto físico, expresión diabólica y tendencia al buen humor del otro.» [1]

The novel is divided into two distinct parts. The main section deals with a group of dissipated *señoritos,* who with several prostitutes are going up the high mountains on the border between Asturias and León to watch an eclipse. The excursion is only an excuse for an orgy. Chapter two, on the other hand, is a flashback to the Arcadian past of the prostitute Rosina in a small fishing village on the Cantabrian coast. This second chapter stands out in sharp contrast to the corruption of the brothels of the big city, Pilares, and to the debauched life of the *señoritos.*

The only *señorito* who is aware of his natural surroundings and who is affected by the eclipse is Alberto Díaz de Guzmán, the protagonist of Pérez de Ayala's first four novels:

> Con esta novela inicia Pérez de Ayala su etapa inicial, compuesta de cuatro novelas ... Se trata de obras parcialmente autobiográficas, que presentan la crisis de conciencia de un joven intelectual, sensible y artista, al chocar con la realidad que le rodea. Así pues ... debe ya retenerse el doble plano (subjetivismo y crítica social) en que se moverán estas novelas. [2]

Alberto stands out in contrast to the other *señoritos* just as Rosina stands out in contrast to the other prostitutes in that she has an essential innocence which one suspects will never become depraved —the prostitute with the soul of a virgin that will appear so frequently in later works.

---

[1] EMILIO FRECHILLA DÍAZ, «Procedimientos narrativos en *Tinieblas en las cumbres*», in *Homenaje a Ramón Pérez de Ayala,* ed. MARÍA DEL CARMEN BOBES NAVES (Oviedo: Gráficas Summa, 1980), p. 78.

[2] AMORÓS, *La novela intelectual,* p. 84.

In the above quotation, Amorós has mentioned the social criticism implicit in this novel. This is manifested in the subtle antithesis between the buffoonery and debauchery —«eat, drink, and be merry»— that takes place during this trip up the mountains and the real emptiness and dreariness of these young people's lives. Another contrast in the novel is in the language and style:

> La pedantería juvenil alcanza su cumbre en las citas clásicas, algunas de ellas incluso en alfabeto griego, que fueron suprimidas después. No se puede olvidar, sin embargo, que todo esto aparece contrapesado por el lirismo de la naturaleza y el desgarro, asturianismos, léxico popular y expresiones vulgares. Este contraste constituye, a mi modo de ver, el ingrediente fundamental en la tonalidad de la novela y es necesario apreciarlo irónicamente para comprenderla en su justo valor. [3]

In other words, the language itself is used to establish the duality between the ideal and the real world.

The general dualities in the novel can thus be summarized: 1) a division between the natural and innocent life in the village of Arenales and the vice and corruption of Pilares; 2) the contrast between the sensitive and meditative Alberto and his merry companions; 3) the difference in Rosina that isolates her from the other prostitutes; 4) the social criticisms implied amidst the merrymaking; and 5) the range of the lexicon itself, from a highly elevated style to one of crude realism. I shall now undertake a more detailed study of the dualities in the novel.

In the story of Rosina, she has to fight off the advances of her employer, Emeterio Barros. The scene is depicted as the struggle between two forces, man against woman:

> Hasta entonces, ni el uno ni la otra habían dicho palabra. Todo el tiempo que duró la lucha habían estado con caudal de energías atento a su fin: el uno a vencer, la otra a rechazar, avaros entrambos de todo esfuerzo inútil; escuchábanse tan solo algún jadeo de momentánea debilidad en la moza y un opaco rugido de ansia en el hombre. [4]

Her union with Fernando, however, is of quite a different nature. In it, Pérez de Ayala seems to imply the Platonic idea of the union of two halves of the same soul:

> El guapo mozo, gallardo y amante, no era, en su imaginación, un advenedizo, sino antigua camarada de niñez; el su mirar rendido como el su sonreír afable

---

[3] AMORÓS, Introduction to *Tinieblas en las cumbres,* by Ramón Pérez de Ayala (Madrid: Clásicos Castalia, 1971), p. 29.

[4] RAMÓN PÉREZ DE AYALA, *Obras completas,* ed. José García Mercadal (Madrid: Aguilar, 1964), I: 41. All subsequent references to the novels of Pérez de Ayala will be to this edition and will be indicated within the body of the text by volume and page numbers in parentheses, except for *A.M.D.G.* which was not included and therefore will be quoted from another edition.

los tenía ella en el alma desde muy antiguo, tal vez desde los ingenuos divertimientos infantiles. Sentíase maridada a él por íntima y misteriosa hermandad, por una fuerza confusa que la arrastraba, a pesar suyo, como a hoja seca el viento invisible. (I, 62)

Later, after serving her first client, Rosina comes to the conclusion that the same act (i.e., copulation) can be dualistic:

Cuando estuvo a solas y consideró su aventura, en fuerza de sutilizar sobre ella y compararla con la de la noche memorable, aquilatando sus diferencias, vino a dar en la certidumbre de que eran cosas de distinta y hasta contradictoria naturaleza y sustancia, y si la una endulzaba y hacía amable la vida, la otra pudiera ayudar a ella como oficio mecánico. (I, 97)

There are other minor touches of dualism, some not without humor, as in the following: «A todo esto [the lovemaking of Rosina and Fernando], los ronquidos feroces del padre de Rosina hacían retumbar la casa con su música horrenda, que era para los dos mozos música celestial» (I, 68). There is also the scene in which the fisherman beats his daughter because she refuses to marry Barros and «el cerdo, poseído de temor, mezclaba a los lamentos de las viejas gruñidos cobardes» (p. 32). As Pelayo H. Fernández has pointed out, giving the pig human qualities emphasizes the inhumanity of the father. [5] When Rosina discovers that she is pregnant and is considering suicide, she has the choice of two cemeteries: «En los pequeños pueblos de la costa cantábrica hay dos cementerios: el religioso, que está adosado a la iglesiuca, por lo común, y el civil, por decirlo así, que es el mar» (I, 82).

Rosina does not commit suicide. Her maternal instincts impel her to go on living and so she goes to Pilares where, after the birth of her baby, she becomes a prostitute. Yet, even as a prostitute, she never loses the innocence and gentleness that are part of her very nature and which only Alberto, because he is different from his companions, is able to notice and appreciate. He is a sensitive, thinking individual whose awareness of death has made him seek immortality as an artist (I, 192).

En esta novela, en concreto, Alberto se singulariza de sus compañeros porque es el único que tiene ojos para la naturaleza. En su carácter «natural» reside el gran atractivo de Rosina. Si Ayala critica a la religión es precisamente porque la ve como algo antinatural, como un oponerse sistemáticamente a las fuerzas e instintos naturales. [6]

Alberto is the only one of the group to be affected by the eclipse, that «efímera cópula» of two polar forces of nature, his majesty the sun and

[5] PELAYO H. FERNÁNDEZ, *Estudios sobre Ramón Pérez de Ayala* (Oviedo: Imprenta «La Cruz», 1978), p. 19.
[6] AMORÓS, Introduction to *Tinieblas*, p. 32.

her majesty the moon (I, 208). But, because of his religious conscience, he is unable to transcend himself and become one with nature, and he cries out in anguish: «—¡Espíritu Misterioso, Ciega y Terrible Potencia, seas quien fueses: piedad para este guiñapo de carne efímera y bestezuela inmundamente orgullosa!... Tengo miedo, tengo miedo» (I, 214). Instead he is thrown into despair:

> Para Alberto, que ha subido a la cumbre (por la sensibilidad, su inteligencia, el cultivo del arte, etc.) el universo está en tinieblas. Busca su sentido y no lo halla. Después de ascender trabajosamente, caerá en la negrura total del eclipse. [7]

Hence, the paradox of the title: one would think that from the peaks, one would be able to see most clearly but, on the contrary, that is precisely when the world, and Alberto, are thrown back into a primeval «niebla». Upon his descent from the «cumbres», Alberto will have the difficult task of becoming «nada menos que todo un hombre» and that will be the subject of the novel that follows this one in sequence (although not in date of publication), *La pata de la raposa*.

There is another important contrast in the description of nature. When Alberto is on top of the mountain, he notices that, to the south, everything is desolate and taciturn; to the north, there is an exuberance of vegetation and color (I, 205). Amorós says of this passage:

> No creo que sea forzar mucho las cosas el ver, detrás de esta referencia geográfica, un propósito simbólico más o menos soterrado. Estamos, sí, en el linde de Asturias y Castilla, pero también —para el joven Pérez de Ayala— en el de dos Españas: la norteña, verde y atractiva, y la meridional, áspera, tradicional y de perfiles rigurosamente quebrados. [8]

This dichotomy between Asturias and León/Castilla appears frequently in the novels of our writer and brings to mind Unamuno's idea of «disociación» which he thinks is caused by the starkness of the Castilian landscape. Pérez de Ayala, trained by the Jesuits and immersed in the Spanish classics, may have had an intellect that saw things dualistically but his Asturian heart cried out for the sweetness of a nature bursting with life.

For Pérez de Ayala, the most antinatural places in the world were the two Jesuit schools he attended as a boarder for six years, from the age of eight to fourteen. The experiences in those schools left their mark forever on his personality. As already mentioned, *A.M.D.G.*, published next in 1910, does not follow *Tinieblas* chronologically, as does *La pata de la raposa*. Instead, it is a prolonged flashback to Alberto Díaz de Guzmán's childhood experiences in a Jesuit school. It is a bitter book, perhaps the least literary

---

[7] AMORÓS, Introduction to *Tinieblas*, p. 34.
[8] AMORÓS, *La novela intelectual*, p. 111.

of the tetralogy. Ayala seems to have felt a need to purge himself of dark memories. Nevertheless, it is an important work because it sheds much light on the personality of Alberto and, hence, on that of Pérez de Ayala himself.

The title page of *A.M.D.G.* contains two quotations, one from Voltaire and the second from Euripides. The Euripides quote says: «La lengua ha jurado, el alma no ha jurado.» Hence, from the start, we have the dualism of duplicity or hypocrisy. That will be the main thrust of the book—the duplicity of the Jesuits who preach Christian charity but are cruel and sadistic, and who gloss over purely material interests with spiritual rationalizations. Most of all, Pérez de Ayala criticizes the Jesuits for considering morally acceptable any act, no matter how materialistic or cruel, if it accomplishes their purposes in what they see as service to God.

Near the beginning of the book, the Jesuits want to build a school and, in order to extract money from a rich widow, they choose Padre Sequeros to be her spiritual counselor. Sequeros is a handsome, virile priest in appearance, although in spirit he is an ascetic and something of a mystic —a perfect combination to seduce old ladies. There is no doubt about the implicit sexuality of this spiritual seduction, and Sequeros himself feels slightly disturbed when the widow finally dies and leaves «seis millones de reales» for the school. He is aware that he has been used somehow and that these are ill-gotten gains, but he is so innocent that he cannot understand his own presentiments. He is also so accustomed to obeying that it is easy for the Father Superior to convince him that what he did was meritorious: «Sequeros tiene el rostro bañado en luz interior: —¡Ad Majorem Dei Gloriam!» [9]

Like *Tinieblas en las cumbres,* the novel starts with a pair of contrasting persons who are also good friends: Gonzalfáñez is rich whereas Dorín, his friend, is poor. Nevertheless, they seem to have been close friends since childhood. Another pair of contrasting friends is the young Alberto and Coste. Bertuco, all sensitivity and intelligence, is the best student in his class, although not always the best behaved. For this reason, he is named «emperador» (after the Roman emperors), but he is not awarded a «dignidad», a prize given at the end of school for good behavior. This does not bother him:

> Bertuco nunca había obtenido una *dignidad,* ni por ellas se le daba una higa. Buena conducta y talento son incompatibles, pensaba. *Dignidades* eran siempre muchachos de inteligencia roma ... para quienes las abundantes horas de estudio resultaban escasas aún, y así, tras de voluntarioso machaqueo, llegaban al aula con las lecciones a medio saber. ... A Bertuco bastábale y sobrábale, para ir a la cabeza de sus compañeros, con la explicación previa que el profesor hacía después de haber señalado la lección...

[9] RAMÓN PÉREZ DE AYALA, *A.M.D.G.*, ed. Andrés Amorós (Madrid: Ediciones Cátedra, 1983), p. 128. All subsequent references to this novel will be from this edition and will be cited by page number in parenthesis within the body of the text.

> ¡Bah! La dignidad... Harto adivinaba Bertuco que la dignidad no la da el
> empleo, sino el mérito; no la otorga la voluntad ajena, sino que es virtud
> inmanente: se tiene o no se tiene; nunca se recibe. (255)

In contrast to Bertuco, Coste never could receive the title of «emperador» and certainly not a «dignidad». His main preoccupation seems to be
eating great quantities of food. He cannot sit still a minute and, as a result,
is constantly being punished. Nonetheless, he is fiercely loyal and honest.
In short, Coste is a healthy, rebellious young boy, uninterested in learning
and incapable of metaphysical speculations. Bertuco is the extreme of intellectual sensitivity whereas Coste is the example of youthful liveliness.
Neither extreme could fit into the Jesuit mold, and this inability to adapt
results in the tragic death of Coste, followed by the illness of Bertuco and
his loss of faith.

The previous summer had been particularly important for the young
Bertuco because, at age fourteen, he had his first sexual experience with
Rosaura, the gardener's daughter. Pérez de Ayala implies that this should
have been a natural event but that religious condemnation of such experiences caused the boy to feel terror of eternal damnation: «¡Tenía ya ma-
licia! El demonio le había iniciado en el gran secreto que rige el mundo» (145). Moreover, when Bertuco discovers «el gran secreto» (revealed
to him by a mocking young seminarian), he feels great revulsion:

> Comenzó a dudar de la sabiduría del omnipotente, que había dispuesto para
> la propagación de la especie acto tan torpe y puerco, y no un arbitrio más
> decoroso y amable. Sintió repugnancia de sus progenitores y desprecio de sí
> propio, considerando su bajo y vergonzoso origen. ... Pero todo su ser aspiraba
> hacia la hembra. (146)

The point is that something so natural should not be treated as a great
sin, and this is where Pérez de Ayala most severely criticizes the Jesuits
and, by extension, Spanish society. (He will later dedicate a two-part novel,
Luna de miel, luna de hiel/Los trabajos de Urbano y Simona, to an extensive study of this subject.) The human and spiritual elements within
man should not be placed in antithetical positions but, rather, both should
be seen as part of a whole.

The difficulty lies in the fact that Christianity is so dualistic:

> De ese peculiar dualismo ... de un lado como fenómeno vital y de otro lado
> como fenómeno cultural, resulta un doble imperativo por el que ha de ser
> regido [el hombre]. Conocemos desde luego el imperativo cultural: para el
> pensamiento, la *verdad*; para la voluntad, la *bondad*; para el sentimiento, la
> *belleza*. Son los imperativos objetivos. Con sólo ellos, sometido sólo a ellos
> el fenómeno cultural, iríamos a dar a la actitud racionalista: una verdad, una
> bondad y una belleza sin conexión con la vida del individuo. A la larga por un
> lado iría la cultura toda, y por otro lado iría la vida del individuo. Es lo que
> a diario se advierte, por ejemplo, en el orden moral. Tenemos una moral de
> ideales perfectos, de una bondad absoluta, pero de unos ideales y de una bon-

dad que nos dejan fríos: ideales y bondad sin arraigo vital y contra los cuales la vida acaba por rebelarse, si no en público, en privado; si no en la acción, en el deseo y en la intención. Una moral tan perfecta, en fin, que obliga al hombre a vivir en constante insinceridad consigo mismo. Una moral, pues, que a fuerza de ser moral y perfecta, acaba por ser imperfecta e inmoral. [10]

The fears of Father Sequeros, the most loving of the teachers, are apparent as he looks upon his students:

El padre Sequeros derramaba una turbia mirada de misericordia sobre todos ellos; los escrutaba luego con ahínco, como si se esforzase en descifrar vagos enigmas. «¿Qué ha sido de ellos? ¿Qué sería de ellos?», se decía. Su destino humano no le inquietaba, sino la eterna solución de aquellas vidas. «¿Cuántos se salvarán? ¿Cuántos se condenarán?» Y le tomaba un temblor de espanto. (143)

In other words, Father Sequeros seems to think that some will inevitably be saved and others will be damned; he does not seem to consider the possibility that all could be saved, or even that all are worth saving. This, then, is the religious and intellectual background of the Alberto Díaz de Guzmán whom we met in *Tinieblas en las cumbres*, and it may explain his tremendous fear when the eclipse darkened the world. Natural phenomena and worldly pursuits are seen as implacable enemies of moral salvation.

The novel may also explain Pérez de Ayala's own preoccupation with dualism and the anguish that this dualistic view of the universe can cause. He was too intelligent, even as a child, not to be aware of the contradictions between what the Jesuits preached and what they did, how they seemed to divide the world into two kinds of human beings: themselves and the rest of humanity, [11] and, finally, that classifications are antinatural: «[With classifications], we describe and explain the world; we make it explicit. But implicitly, in nature herself, there are no classes.» [12] As Amorós has summed it up:

Leyendo esta novela, toda persona de buena voluntad siente la pena de que Pérez de Ayala no hubiera podido conocer, de niño, otro tipo de religiosidad distinta en el que —por ejemplo— las cosas naturales fueran testimonio de la grandeza divina y no enemigos implacables. [13]

Up in the darkness of that eclipse, Alberto loses the last ray of hope for artistic glory he had kept hidden deep in his heart. All ideals are now

---

[10] CÉSAR BARJA, *Libros y autores contemporáneos* (Madrid: Librería General de Victoriano Suárez 1935), p. 194.

[11] JOSÉ GARCÍA MERCADAL, Prologue to *Obras completas* by RAMÓN PÉREZ DE AYALA, p. xlvi.

[12] WATTS, p. 49.

[13] AMORÓS, *La novela intelectual*, p. 140.

gone and, with them, his sense of identity. One solution is to take the way of the libertine: «Bebe, come, fornica, corónate de rosas» (I, 222), but in the end, he is too sensitive for that. He must create a new identity for himself, and this he sets out to do in the next novel, *La pata de la raposa*.

What seems to have taken away Alberto's will is the awareness of death and damnation drummed into him in the Jesuit schools. It interferes with his living life to the fullest:

> La clave de todo esto radica en la muerte: «si se sabe inculcar bien en el espíritu el torcedor de la muerte, no hay modo ya de recuperar el amor a la acción ni la espontaneidad y descuido de los goces terrenos». ... La tesis exactamente opuesta es la que expondrá Ayala al comentar el título de su siguiente novela, *La pata de la raposa*: los pueblos y los individuos fuertes se olvidan de la muerte y marchan hacia delante, con un vitalismo activo y emprendedor. [14]

The most important aspect of the novel, therefore, will be the antithesis between *voluntad* and *abulia*. Alberto wavers constantly between the two. First, he is aware that his cultural training has robbed him of life. In seeking to cure himself, he throws out all his books, breaks up his statues, destroys his paintings—but he is not entirely successful for he is unable to destroy the Mona Lisa. Then he decides to go out to his country home to live the simple life—«hay que animalizarse» (I, 262). His mentors will be two dogs, a cat, and a rooster. Azor is his country dog, brave and fierce; Sultán is his city dog, «cortesano y medroso». Alberto breaks one of Azor's legs because the dog, not recognizing his master, attacks when Alberto tries to enter the farmhouse. After the leg heals, Alberto decides to teach his dog tricks. He seems to be trying to prove to himself that life is still worth living despite physical or spiritual handicaps:

> Y desde aquel punto se aplicó a convertir a *Azor* en un perro sabio y acróbata. El animal se prestaba a todo de buen grado, si bien el aprendizaje era prolijo y penoso. Con lo cual perro y amo ganaban: *Azor*, en habilidad; Alberto, en instinto... (I, 265)

But Alberto is unable to escape his intellectual background. In a tavern where some miners are drinking, he looks at the scene and at the drinkers through the eyes of the various artists he has studied, and he compares the songs he hears to Grieg and Rimsky-Korsakov. In short, he feels alienated from his surroundings; he looks at everything from an esthetic distance:

> ¡Cándido de mí! He aquí que me apercibo a gozar por primera vez de las cosas, como si hubieran sido creadas sólo para mí, ¿y qué ha sucedido? Que no veo con mis ojos ni oigo con mis oídos. La realidad permanece ajena y misteriosa para mí. Entre ella y yo se interponen las imágenes y las sensacio-

[14] AMORÓS, *La novela intelectual*, p. 139.

nes experimentadas por otros sentidos que no son los de mi cuerpo. No he visto la taberna, ni el paisaje, ni a los mineros, ni al chigrero; tampoco he oído el canto de la moza con la música del acordeón. Los han visto y oído por mí Jordaens, Teniers, Verrochio, Lysipo, Grieg, Rimsky-Korsakov, y por ahí adelante. ¡Maldito esteticismo! ... ¿Soy un hombre o soy un portfolio de estampas, con sendas inscripciones muertas al pie? Sólo la fruición del tacto ha sido exclusivamente mía; y la del olfato...; y la del paladar. Tacto, olfato y paladar, que no son sentidos estéticos, sino sentidos animales. Hay que animalizarse. ... Y dar comienzo de nuevo, dentro de mí mismo, a la historia humana... (I, 262)

He goes to visit Fina, and they exchange their first kiss. As in the union of Rosina and Fernando, there is a spiritual as well as physical union between the lovers: «Alberto, además de la sensación espiritual de transporte y abandono, gozaba el deleite físico de los labios de Fina, duros, tersos, fríos, húmedos y castos» (I, 302). Later that evening, however, he is dragged to a house of prostitution by Telesforo, the fiancé of Fina's sister, Leonor. Afterwards, Alberto feels deep revulsion for himself. He has profaned the purity of Fina's love and, seeing this profanation in terms of either/or, he is overcome by anguish:

Hallábase Alberto a campo abierto, en la carretera de Pilares. Sobre el polvo mate del camino brillaban los rieles de acero del tranvía, paralelamente. *Atraído por ellos, Alberto comenzó a andar, siguiendo el centro de la vía.* Aquellas dos rectas que se hundían en una penumbra cercana y que nunca se habían de unir le martirizaban, inculcándole desesperados presentimientos: Fina y él. «Estoy perdido», se dijo. (I, 317—emphasis is mine)

What causes the anguish is the absolute division into categories between the dualism of two lines running forever parallel, with man caught in the middle:

Good and evil are abstract categories like up and down, and categories do not perform their function unless they are kept distinct. It is thus perfectly proper that the *concepts* of good and evil be distinct, dualistic and irreconcilable, that they be as firm and clear as any other measure. The «problem of duality» arises only when the abstract is confused with the concrete, when it is thought that there are as clearly distinguishable entities in the natural universe. [15]

Unable to face Fina, Alberto breaks with her. However, he also writes a poem divided into two parts in which he seems to be searching for an excuse for his actions. The first part deals with a prostitute; the second is a series of sophisticated explanations of his behavior:

¿Por qué dividió el autor de esta composición en dos partes, y la dramatizó, desdoblándose en dos personas? Quizá el propio Alberto no se dio cuenta,

[15] WATTS, p. 17.

obedeciendo al instinto de bifurcación que en tales crisis escinde el corazón humano en dos porciones; llora la una de vergüenza y la otra, sofisticándose a sí propia, fingiendo comprensiva entereza, ríe y supone que así expulsa de su vecindad inseparable aquella porción dolida, su mitad, que ha padecido rebajamiento indeleble. (I, 324)

Abruptly Alberto decides to join a troup of wandering acrobats, the same circus that brought Fernando to Rosina's village. This is a return to the problem of esthetic distance, the duality between living life and feelings intensely, and observing oneself living them: «Nuestro inquieto protagonista ha decidido tomar la vida como espectáculo y convertirse él mismo en espectáculo, tal las pantominas que representa en el circo.» [16] Pérez de Ayala uses the image of the mirror to show Alberto's alienation from himself:

Con un gesto muy repetido en las novelas de Ayala ... Alberto se mira al espejo. (Igual hacía él mismo en *Tinieblas*; igual hará Urbano en *Las novelas de Urbano y Simona*.) No se reconoce a sí mismo. Es un intelectual que se desdobla; no logra la unidad consigo mismo ni, por consiguiente, una adecuada relación con el mundo. Ve siempre una distancia entre él y los demás, no rompe nunca sus límites. Y, lo que es peor, percibe también una distancia interna, en lo hondo de sí mismo. Alberto se plantea dramáticamente la oposición entre ensimismamiento y enajenación. [17]

The cause of Alberto's alienation from himself is his intellectual and social formation which is *antivital*:

El problema que nos plantea Alberto ... es el de saber en qué medida se puede retornar a un yo puro después de haber sufrido el influjo social, y en qué medida también se mantiene fresco y vivo ese yo puro luego de revestirse con la costra de lo social. [18]

«La razón mata», as Unamuno said, and Alberto, in spite of his great efforts to forge an identity for himself, simply cannot break the habit of esthetic distance. He is unable to integrate either with himself, his surroundings, or even with Fina, who might have saved him. Fina says she knows nothing of the things of the world; however, she does know the most important thing: «Porque ya te digo, no sé nada de las cosas del mundo. Una sé, y es cosa mía; lo único —púdicamente inclinó la cabeza» (I, 299). What Fina comprehends is love, the one great unifying force of the universe.

The two sisters, Fina and Leonor, are a contrasting pair:

Leonor, la primera, fue desde muy niña vivaracha, desenvuelta, mimosa. Josefina, por el contrario, era taciturna, meditativa y poco afectuosa exterior-

---

[16] FERNÁNDEZ, *Estudios sobre Ramón Pérez de Ayala*, p. 92.

[17] AMORÓS, *La novela intelectual*, pp. 170-71. This opposition between the lyrical «ensimismamiento» and the dramatic «enajenación» will be treated in greater depth in *Troteras y danzaderas* and again in *Belarmino y Apolonio*.

[18] FERNÁNDEZ, *Estudios sobre Ramón Pérez de Ayala*, p. 83.

mente. Los padres amaban más a Leonor y se enorgullecían de su hermosura...
A Josefina la habían habituado a considerarse fea... (I, 281)

However, Fina's external behavior is not a true picture of her real self.
Seemingly cold and aloof, she is actually a sensual woman, as her response
to nature shows: «La canción clara del arroyo le acariciaba los oídos, y el
olor de tanta rosa la mantenía con los labios y los dientes entreabiertos,
jadeando un poco» (I, 292). At first Alberto treats Josefina like a child, as
does her family, but, «poco a poco, Alberto fue comprendiendo que la
supuesta niña guardaba un arcano interior, profundo y rico» (I, 284). Alberto falls in love with her but seems incapable of making a total commitment because he has a tendency to see her in purely esthetic terms. In a
letter to his friend Juan Halconete (who Andrés Amorós thinks is Azorín),
Alberto says that Fina is like a Gothic statue («belleza cristiana, ... belleza
moral») as opposed to Greek statues which emphasize movement. In addition, he points out, Greek statues are never virgins or mothers, whereas

> el arquetipo de la mujer cristiana es la virgen madre; sublime paradoja. Y tal
> es el linaje de belleza de Fina. Con ser sutil e infantil, ... sugiere no sé qué
> densa impresión de apta maternidad presunta; y estoy cierto que, en siendo
> madre, envolverá a quienes al lado suyo vivan, en fresco aliento de virginidad
> incólume. (I, 339)

Julio Cejador, who had been Pérez de Ayala's teacher and who left the
Jesuit order just as Father Atienza does in *A.M.D.G.*, made this interesting
observation about his pupil with regard to women:

> Tocando hasta las más traspuestas fibras de su alma, tengo que decir que
> Ramón tiene un temperamento arrebatado y abierto, que se deja arrastrar al
> amor por la belleza ingenua y sencilla y por la bondad de los sentimientos de
> la mujer. Se enamora y se deja prender en las redes mujeriles en cuanto alguna
> vislumbre de belleza o de bondad atrae sus ojos. Pero son tan nobles sus sentimientos, que no le dejan gozar sosegadamente del amor puramente lascivo;
> en medio del placer su alma se levanta a cosas mayores, compadécese de la
> desgraciada y todo el ímpetu carnal se convierte en compasión de maestro, de
> padre, de protector, y acaba trasminando sus propios elevados sentires en el
> cieno más asqueroso de la más ruin mujercilla. Sus mismos amoríos desinteresados y nada carnales con personas de su clase, sus noviazgos, hablando en
> castellano, no duran con el mismo fervor, se enfrían y recalientan a tiempos,
> merced al vaivén de sus pensamientos y sentimientos estéticos, que le arroban
> y le hacen despreciable todo lo que no sea arte, o le afirman más en el cariño
> haciéndole ver arte y bellezas estéticas en su amada. [19]

It seems obvious that all of the above contradictory feelings also describe
Alberto Díaz de Guzmán.

Telesforo Hurtado, who eventually marries Leonor, forms a contrast to
Alberto. Telesforo talks about love in lofty terms as the purest spiritual

[19] CEJADOR, pp. 246-47.

sentiment, yet it is he who insists on going to a house of prostitution immediately after the two men have visited their fiancées. Hurtado makes a
clear distinction between the spiritual love he professes to feel for Leonor
and the desires of the flesh «para pasar el rato». In Alberto's concept, love
is a union of both the body and the spirit: «La censura de Pérez de Ayala
recae sobre esta disociación del amor en dos orbes independientes; a recon-
ciliar los dos en una síntesis armónica se encaminarán sus *Novelas de Urbano y Simona*.» [20]

Hurtado eventually abandons his wife and runs off with a French singer
(and Alberto's money). Ayala is critical of the double standard that considers
such actions so natural in a man that society readily excuses him and his
wife accepts his adultery with «absurda sumisión». [21] Yet, as Pelayo H. Fernández has noticed, there is another and unexpected side to Leonor's
character:

> En otro plano, la huida de Telesforo muestra una faceta desconocida hasta
> ahora en la personalidad de Leonor. Incapaz de admitir la realidad en toda su
> crudeza, sublima el amor y el carácter de su marido. La que nos había impre-
> sionado como coqueta y superficial, adquiere tonos dulces de criatura ideal. [22]

Pérez de Ayala is abandoning the relatively flat characterizations of his
earlier novels. Even Alberto and Rosina are not complex in *Tinieblas,* but
they become more so as the tetralogy progresses. Rosina, especially, develops
into a very enigmatic character in *Troteras y danzaderas*. But in *La pata de
la raposa,* even relatively minor characters, like Leonor, show contradictory
sides to their personality. These complications will become even more
intense in his later novels.

Another contradictory character in the novel is Meg, the antithesis of
Fina: «Frente al 'buen amor' de Fina, Meg es ejemplo del 'loco amor',
apasionado y engañoso, que destruye la armonía vital de los hombres en vez
de favorecerla.» [23] Alberto does not know what to make of Meg. What
disconcerts him is his inability to conceive of the fact that evil can exist
in a form so beautiful: «Alberto miró a Meg con angustia; se estremecía
pensando que un cuerpo tan fino y hermoso pudiera albergar un día un
alma mala» (I, 380). Alberto has been drawn to Meg by a purely physical
attraction. As soon as he discovers her relations with the young Ettore, he
retreats immediately into the cold esthetic distance that is his protection
against emotions:

> Había asumido instantáneamente un estado de aplomo espiritual. Sus ideas
> y sentimientos adoptaban de nuevo la impasible serenidad estética. De actor de

[20] AMORÓS, *La novela intelectual*, p. 189.
[21] AMORÓS, *La novela intelectual*, p. 189.
[22] FERNÁNDEZ, *Estudios sobre Ramón Pérez de Ayala*, p. 96.
[23] AMORÓS, *La novela intelectual*, p. 187.

la tragedia..., se había convertido en espectador... y ahora estaba en la margen, tranquilo y sonriente, no contemplando en aquel raudo torbellino otra cosa que el juego de bellas fuerzas naturales... Meg ya no era sino un objeto curioso de observación y un interesante tema artístico; había descendido de tirana a esclava... (I, 461-62)

But Pérez de Ayala does not censure Meg, nor does Alberto—she is as she is for reasons perhaps too complex to understand. We are beginning to deal now with the complexity of perspectives that will preoccupy the author in his later novels:

Tita Anastasia permanece meditabunda. Dice luego [a Alberto]:

—Usted dice que todo es guapo, que es lo mismo que decir que todo es feo. Usted dice que todo está bien, que es lo mismo que decir que todo está mal. Usted dice que para conocer la verdad hay que lavarse las manos, y esto se me figura que es lo mismo que decir que no se puede conocer la verdad. Y usted no va a misa, que es lo mismo que no creer en Dios. Y, sin embargo, me parece usted un santín... ¡No me lo explico!...

—Ahí está el *quid,* tita Anastasia. Todo es cuestión del cómo...; y además el cuándo y el para qué. Si conociéramos el cómo, cuándo y para qué, la cosa más fea puede ser hermosa, y la cosa más mala puede ser buena, y en efecto lo son, cuando lo son para lo que propiamente son, o existen, pues por algo y para algo existen, *entóncenes* conoceríamos toda la verdad, y, claro está seríamos como Dioses...

Pero la vieja no le oye. Está absorta en sus cavilaciones; dentro de su espíritu hay el malestar de una contradicción que nunca atinará a resolver. (I, 436-37)

After his experiences with Meg, Alberto tries to go back to Fina, but it is too late—she is dead and the novel ends. Without the love that could have saved him, it must be assumed that Alberto never is able to integrate his personality, that he continues to look at the world through the eyes of an artist, rather than feeling the world as a man, and that he remains an *abúlico.*

The story of Alberto Díaz de Guzmán ends with this novel and Fina's death. The novel that was published a year later (1913) covers a period of three years during which Alberto was separated from Fina and living the life of a bohemian in Madrid. One assumes that this is just before his experience with Meg. In this novel, *Troteras y danzaderas,* Alberto is almost completely *abúlico* (although he does manage to write a novel) and we are told that he has broken with his fiancée although we are not told why. In fact, Alberto is no longer the central figure in this novel; the more interesting character is Teófilo Pajares, although the real protagonist is the whole group of poets, playwrights, singers, dancers, and intellectuals who were active in Madrid in December, 1910. [24]

[24] Date established by Amorós in his study of *Troteras y danzaderas.*

Although the theme of the sensitive *abúlico* versus the life-force man continues (Teófilo versus Fernando), the main interest here is the distinction made between *el espíritu lírico* and *el espíritu dramático*. *El espíritu lírico* is the ability to feel life intensely, not only one's own, but also the emotions of other people. *El espíritu dramático,* on the other hand, consists of that esthetic distance already mentioned in which the person contemplates himself and others from a safe distance, from the point of view of a spectator rather than a participant.

Perhaps the most famous scene in *Troteras y danzaderas* is the one in which Alberto reads *Othello* to Verónica. The uneducated girl has never heard of the play and therefore she has no preconceived notions which may influence her reactions. As she listens, she becomes more and more involved in the feelings of all the characters, first siding with Iago, then with Othello, then with Desdemona's father, and back and forth. In the end, she forgets that it is a play, and, fearing for Desdemona's life, she grabs the book and begs Alberto to stop so that Desdemona will not have to die. For Pérez de Ayala, Verónica's reactions prove that *Othello* is a great tragedy and not just a good melodrama:

> De la emoción lírica había trascendido Verónica a la emoción dramática, de la tragedia del hombre interno a la tragedia de los hombres entre sí; y así como en el primer acto había sentido que, en el misterio de su alma, todo hombre es justo y bueno, aun el que no lo parece, porque sus intenciones y conducta se rigen por sutiles impulsos, a manera de leyes necesarias, así también ahora Verónica presentía que los sucesos que entretejen la historia y de la cual los hombres reciben placer, dolor, exaltación, gloria, ruina, son como tienen que ser, producto de elementos fatales en proporciones fatales. (I, 576)

Tragedy, as opposed to melodrama, treats all the characters with understanding and compassion, and their actions are justified; thus tragedy pits goodness against goodness. Melodrama, on the contrary, pits goodness against evil, the hero against the villain. The first produces catharsis; the second engenders sentimentality. Therefore, Alberto concludes, the difference between great and inferior art is not a question of technique but, rather, of moral conception (I, 576-77). The end result of the cathartic experience is that the spectator feels a sense of justice and tolerance:

> —Digo que aquella catarsis no es más, si bien se mira, que acto preparatorio del corazón para recibir dignamente el advenimiento de dos grandes virtudes... la tolerancia y la justicia...
> —Estas dos virtudes no se sienten; por tanto, no se transmiten, a no ser que el creador de la obra artística posea de consuno espíritu lírico y espíritu dramático, los cuales, fundidos, forman el espíritu trágico. El espíritu lírico equivale a la capacidad de subjetivación... El espíritu dramático, por el contrario, es la capacidad de impersonalidad... El campo de acción del espíritu lírico es el hombre; el del espíritu dramático es la Humanidad. Y de la resolución de estos dos esprítus, que parecen antitéticos, surge la tragedia. (I, 735-36)

Pérez de Ayala is becoming increasingly conscious of a need for unity, of a «resolución de ... espíritus ... antitéticos». His next important works, *Tres novelas poemáticas,* are essentially tragic, but later, in his last three major novels, he is able to integrate a view of reality into what he called «tragicomedias». (He was a great admirer of Arniches.)

The two prototypes in *Troteras y danzaderas* of the lyric spirit and the dramatic spirit are Verónica and Rosina. Verónica, the embodiment of the lyric spirit, seems to be a paradoxical character. Alberto says to her: «—En ti, Verónica, el entregarse a todos y a todo es en tal grado que de vicio se hace virtud» (I, 583). It so happens that, although she is a prostitute, her sign is Virgo:

> —La mujer nacida por este tiempo —leyó Amparito— será muy honrada, sincera, franca, muy aseada en su persona y de deseos ardientes, modesta en su conversación, afecta a los placeres matrimoniales y fiel a su marido; será también muy buena madre y muy mujer de su casa. (I, 718)

The above qualities are the ideal virtues for a bourgeois wife and mother. There is no doubt here of Pérez de Ayala's irony, but the fact is that Verónica does indeed embody these virtues. She quits prostitution as soon as she is able, having entered the profession only at the insistence of her mother and to help support her brothers and sisters, and she is faithful to Teófilo, nursing him tenderly until he dies, even though he loves another woman. When Travesedo condescendingly asks her to marry him on the very day that Teófilo dies, she refuses his offer, even though it would bring her honor and security. She loves only one man and remains true to him. Instead she goes to the theater to dance that night; she has to keep on working to support her family. The implication is that taking Travesedo's offer would be a subtle kind of prostitution; she would rather make an honest living by dancing. Alberto admires in Verónica her ability to encompass both the lyric and dramatic spirit. She is the most integrated and harmonious character we have seen so far in the tetralogy and this harmony is emphasized by Pérez de Ayala's description of her behavior toward Travesedo:

> Existían vehementes indicios de que Travesedo gustaba mucho de Verónica. La muchacha, que lo había echado de ver, trataba al hombre de las barbas lóbregas con un bien mesurado compás de afecto, equidistante del amor y del desdén. (I, 687)

Verónica is, in short, a woman who can be true to herself, yet understands and sympathizes with the feelings of others.

Rosina is the opposite of Verónica; she represents the dramatic spirit. It is not that she is insensitive or unkind, but her common sense will always win over her feelings. She compares her first experience as a prostitute to her lovemaking with Fernando, and her conclusion is that the two acts are different. Perhaps it is her cold, practical approach to her profession that enables her to succeed in becoming Don Sabas's mistress. Unlike Verónica, Rosina would never go off with an Angelón Ríos and stay in his house two or three days waiting for food and money. Her dramatic spirit makes her want to laugh at poor Teófilo, even though she is flattered by his adoration:

> Tan inesperado fue todo, tan fuerte, que Rosina, a causa del choque y a pesar suyo, se encontró desdoblada en dos personalidades diferentes: la una estaba plenamente dominada por la situación, la otra había salido de fuera, como espectador, y exclamaba casi en arrobo: «¿Es posible que exista amor tan puro, apasionado y rendido?»... Rosina estaba atacada de una breve risa nerviosa que sonaba a sollozos y que por sollozos tomó Pajares. (I, 509)

Fernando is the center of her life. However, one man alone does not satisfy her:

> Rosina consideraba el amor a su hombre, a Fernando, como la necesidad permanente de su vida..., la tierra, la base en donde posarse y reposarse. Fernando era para ella la plenitud de su feminidad, de su sexo, pero, al propio tiempo, necesitaba del amor de Teófilo, lo ansiaba como complemento y realce del otro amor. Un ave ignora que sufre la tiranía de la tierra hasta tanto que no se le entumecen las alas o las pierde; entonces, junto con la nostalgia del vuelo, llega a saber que la tierra es el elemento que la domina, así como el aire es el elemento que se deja dominar. Pues algo semejante le sucedía a Rosina. Con relación a Fernando, se sentía empequeñecida, anulada, entregada sin albedrío a él. Recordando ahora el sumo acatamiento y entrega que de sus potencias Teófilo le había hecho en otro tiempo y la exaltación gozosa y altanera que de aquel amor ella había recibido, ardía en anhelos de resucitar las emociones de entonces. (I, 766-67)

But if she has to make a choice between Teófilo and Fernando, Rosina will choose Fernando. Indeed, it is not even a choice; there is no alternative: «La colisión entre los destinos individuales era irremediable y de ella sale vencedor —no podía ser de otra manera— el más vital, el más fuerte.» [25]

The essential conflict between Teófilo and Fernando is that of the thinker versus the life-force man. The two seem incompatible:

> El poeta... no es un hombre recio, forzudo..., pues sería absurdo concebir que una persona dotada de extrema sensibilidad... sea un bravo y perfecto ejemplar de la raza humana en lo que se refiere a la parte material. No, todo lo contrario; yo doy por sentado... que este hombre es todo espíritu, nada más que espíritu. Y la mujer, inopinadamente, huye de él en compañía de un titiritero, de un hombre todo materia, torpeza e instinto. Este es un drama, si hay dramas en el mundo. (I, 736-37)

---

[25] AMORÓS, *Vida y literatura en «Troteras y danzaderas»* (Madrid: Editorial Castalia, 1973), pp. 246-47.

Rosina has a strong instinct for survival and, for this reason, she will always choose life and strength. On his deathbed, Teófilo says that he understands her choice: «Ha hecho bien, ha hecho bien: Fernando es la fuerza y la vida; yo era un fantasma de ficciones y falsedades, una criatura sin existencia real. Que ha hecho bien y que la perdono» (I, 810). Teófilo has also learned that art is antithetical to life:

> Se cree vulgarmente que el amor estimula el ejercicio de las artes, y muy par-
> ticularmente el de la poesía. Ahora veo que no. Al contrario, le anula a uno.
> Pero es un anulamiento tan placentero... ¿Que ahora no puedo escribir? No
> importa; aguardaré. Tienes razón. La vida es anterior y superior al arte. Yo
> ahora vivo. (I, 791)

Teófilo is the most interesting personality in this novel. He is the first of those characters that will henceforth recur in Pérez de Ayala's work, a personality made up of such contradictions as to render him absurd, yet treated with a compassion that in the end endears him to the reader more than any other character in this novel. One of the contradictions is that, although he has written poems describing death with morbid delight, the actual thought of his own death from tuberculosis fills him with dread. In his poetry, he has the habit of transforming the prostitutes he encounters into clavichord-playing princesses with alabaster hands. But when he meets Rosina and falls in love with her, he is unable to write. Having hoped to conquer her, he is enslaved by her. He writes poetry about the most sublime subjects, but is concerned about appearing before Rosina in tattered underwear. Teófilo is aware that there are two contradictory natures within him, and therefore he is not surprised when his mother confesses to him that he is the bastard son of a priest:

> —Venga más cerca de mí, madre, que yo la sienta pegada a mí. Así. No
> sabía las circunstancias que usted me ha referido; pero he sentido siempre en
> lo más hondo y arcano de mi ser la certidumbre de que yo había sido engen-
> drado por una mala sangre en una sangre generosa. Siempre ha habido en mí
> dos naturalezas: una torpe y vil, simuladora y vana; otra sincera y leal, entu-
> siasta y dadivosa. (I, 809)

However, as Amorós has pointed out, «¿Qué lector de la novela no podría decir lo mismo?» [26]

Another contradictory element in the novel is an unlikely friendship; as with Coste, Alberto seeks a friend who is the opposite of himself, Angelón Ríos. Angelón is twenty years older than Alberto in physical age, but twenty years younger in spirit. Alberto is delicate; Angelón is robust and has an insatiable lust for life:

[26] AMORÓS, *Vida y literatura*, p. 243.

Alberto admiraba en Angelón... su acometividad en conjunturas difíciles, su carácter de genuino hombre de acción, esto es, fundamentalmente bueno: amaba el mundo y la vida por ser el uno y la otra fértiles en obstáculos. (I, 545)

Throughout *Troteras y danzaderas* there are pairs: two bullfighters, two painters, two Petunias, two actors, two aristocrats, two gamblers. Amorós implies that this is inherent in the Spanish psyche:

Muchos autores —entre ellos, el propio Pérez de Ayala— han comentado que el pueblo español siempre se ha apasionado por... parejas: Galdós o Pereda, Cánovas o Sagasta, «Bombita» o «Machaquito», Joselito o Belmonte..., etcétera. [27]

Implicit in the title of the novel itself and in the chapter titles are paradoxes that merit our attention.

Troteras y danzaderas is taken from a line in *El libro de buen amor*. *Troteras,* a word not readily understood, seems to mean prostitution, perhaps by analogy to Trotaconventos. Rosina is the *trotera* and Verónica is the *danzadera*. When we first meet Rosina in *Tinieblas*, we notice that, though she is a prostitute, she is essentially innocent and probably will remain so. In the later novel, she is not corrupt but her pragmatic, sensible approach to life assures her survival. This materialistic tendency is not to be condemned. Verónica is the *danzadera*—the spirit that lets itself go in Dionysian abandon. Since Verónica does not know how to take care of herself, one wonders what will become of her when she can no longer dance. She will probably become a prostitute again. Rosina, in her place, would never have refused Travesedo's offer of marriage. *Troteras,* then, is the materialistic world and *danzaderas* the spiritual. Both have equal value.

The first chapter is entitled «Sesostris y Platón». Sesostris is a turtle, Platón a fish. Don Sabas, a deep thinker in spite of his being a politician, admires Sesostris because she has a hard shell that protects her; for this reason, the turtle is one of the oldest creatures on earth. Another old creature, the fish, is like man—all epidermis—and therefore very vulnerable. In fact, Angelón eats the fish Platón in one gulp. Sesostris pays little attention to events around her; she just goes her way intent on survival as she eats another very old creature, the cockroach. Don Sabas has named the fish Platón because he thinks his fishbowl is the entire universe. In short, the author establishes a division between the material world (Sesostris) and the ideal world (Platón), and he implies that the material world will survive whereas the ideal world may not.

The second chapter, called «Verónica y Desdémona», is a study of the differences between the lyrical and the dramatic spirit, and between tragedy and melodrama.

---

[27] AMORÓS, *Vida y literatura,* p. 115.

The third chapter, «Troteras y danzaderas», describes the entrance of Rosina and Verónica onto the stage, the first as a singer and the second as a dancer. To be a singer one must have some training and voice control, which Rosina had. This emphasizes her dramatic spirit. The Dionysian Verónica, on the other hand, had no training and therefore she dances as her lyrical instinct leads her, in total abandon, with no forethought or planning.

Also, Verónica as a dancer and Tejero as a philosopher both earn the same «mil quinientas pesetas al mes».[28] If one keeps in mind that most primitive drama originated from the dance, one notices the polarity between philosophy and drama that will be elaborated in *Belarmino y Apolonio*.

In chapter four, «Hermes Trimegisto and Santa Teresa», there is the opposition between occult and Christian mysticism. Lolita seems to combine them; she has a San Antonio de Padua who is supposed to bring her «novios», but she is also very superstitious and tells fortunes with cards. She is from Andalucía and therefore has something of the gypsy in her: nominally Christian, she combines many occult elements in her religious beliefs.

The final chapter, «Ormuzd y Ahrimán», alludes to the Zoroastrian forces that rule the world—Ormuzd is the force of good and Ahrimán the force of evil. The important thing is that they are twin brothers, and their father is Zurban, a word which means fate, fortune and/or time:[29]

> The fact that the pair... are *brothers* intimates that there is still some recognition of the basic unity of the opposed forces. But, in general, as we move Westward from the Indus basin, the common ground between the two drops out of sight, and the conflict begins to be a struggle to the death, fought in absolute seriousness.[30]

In this chapter, the first few pages describe the idyllic life of Rosina, Teófilo, Alberto and Verónica in the small fishing village of Ciluria. Abruptly Rosina returns to Fernando and everything changes; Teófilo gets very ill and dies. The contrast seems to be between the ultimate good (life), and the ultimate evil (death). The implication is that they are both an integral part of the universe, both necessary and equal.

Troteras y danzaderas is the last work that deals with Alberto Díaz de Guzmán. The novel seems to have been finished in Munich in November of 1912. The previous year in Florence, Pérez de Ayala had met Mabel Rick, a young American woman from Allentown, Pennsylvania. Their courtship lasted for two years and, on September 1, 1913, they

---

[28] AMORÓS, *Vida y literatura*, p. 149.
[29] WATTS, p. 142.
[30] WATTS, p. 45.

were married in Allentown. The following year they had their first son. In other words, some very important things were happening in the emotional life of our author; he, who seems to have had a rather loveless childhood far from his mother and father, is now experiencing for the first time the great integrating force of love.

Already between *La pata* and *Troteras* we see a great change in attitude. *La pata* ends with the loss of all hope for the redemption of Alberto; *Troteras* ends with cynicism, but a cynicism that hides a gentle smile of irony. No blame is cast. All is as it should be.

3

TRES NOVELAS POEMÁTICAS DE LA VIDA ESPAÑOLA

Tres novelas poemáticas de la vida española appeared in 1916 and showed a marked change in Pérez de Ayala's style and theme. They are no longer the veiled autobiographies of the tetralogy, but deal, instead, with problems which the author considered of national importance. Moreover, they reveal an author of great erudition who makes conscious allusions to the classical literatures of Greece and Spain. The style of the three short works varies according to the literature the author is attempting to evoke, but they have two things in common: each chapter is prefaced by a short poem which synthesizes the content of that chapter, and all three criticize some aspect of Spanish life. Two *(Luz de domingo* and *La caída de los Limones)* had appeared previously in periodicals but without the poetic prefaces. The poems seem to have been added later in preparation for the first edition of the trilogy.[1]

The most obvious dualistic element in this trilogy is the use of both poetry and prose to develop the same theme. According to Pérez de Ayala, the poems attempt to convey truth «por un procedimiento más directo y sintético que analítico».[2]

> [The] two different modes of language imply two modes of vision. Factual language obviously represents the view of nature which is held to be normal, practical, and sane—the world of science and industry, business and bureaucracy, of hard facts and cold calculations... In different ways the poet, the painter, and the mystic try to describe another world, or rather, this same world of nature seen in another way.[3]

While the mixture of poetry and prose combines synthesis and analysis in order to arrive at a more complete truth, the poems at the same time form a sort of Greek chorus which relate what the narrative will act out. Thus, in addition to the dualism of language, there is also the dualism of

---

[1] Amorós, *La novela intelectual*, p. 236.
[2] G. G. Brown, *A Literary History of Spain. The Twentieth Century* (London: Ernest Benn Ltd., 1972), p. 39.
[3] Watts, pp. 6-7.

spectator-actor so prevalent in Ayala's works. G. G. Brown finds that the Greek chorus poems often function as spectators to the subjective drama taking place in the prose narrative. [4]

«PROMETEO»

It is perhaps these *novelas poemáticas* which show most clearly Pérez de Ayala's concern with «el problema de España» and his ties to the Generation of '98. The dichotomy between the intellect and the instinctual life force continues to preoccupy him, and nowhere is this division more clearly stated than in the first of the three novels, *Prometeo*. This novella incorporates the two Greek myths of Prometheus and Odysseus. Dualism is manifest in the antithetical personalities of the two mythical heroes: Prometheus rebels against the gods; his audacity tends to spectacular deeds such as stealing fire for mankind. Odysseus is crafty, cautious, obedient to the gods, and concerned with very human problems such as going home to free his wife and larder from her parasitic suitors. The former is impulsive and rash; the latter, plodding and tenacious. Marco Setiñano, a self-styled Odysseus with Promethean ambitions, is frustrated because he feels that his intellect keeps him from performing the great deeds he dreams of. He fails to understand what his uncle has tried to explain to him — that Prometheus can touch the heavens only because he has men like Odysseus holding him up: «No creo, como tú, que la Humanidad es ornamento adosado al cielo por la naturaleza semidivina de algunos hombres de excepción. Estos hombres tocan el cielo con la frente porque los demás hombres los aúpan» (II, 611). The Nietzschean superman is thus rejected in favor of the little «hombres frustrados... que son la levadura de la Humanidad» (II, 611) and who make up its «intrahistoria».

As befits a tale dealing with two such mythical heroes, Pérez de Ayala uses the epic style in the poetry and prose of this novella, but the prose epic style has degenerated into parody; modern man no longer has the makings of the mythical hero:

> Así, lo que en las edades épicas fue canto heroico al son de la cítara, es ahora voz muda y gráfica, esto es, palabra escrita, sin otro acompañamiento que la estridencia lánguida de la pluma metálica sobre el papel deleznable. El aeda ha degenerado en novelador. (II, 594)

Moreover, the muse that now inspires is a «diosa cominera de estos días plebeyos, diosa de la curiosidad impertinente y del tedio fisgón, que no

---

[4] BROWN, p. 39.

te gozas si no es hurgando entre las cenizas del hogar ajeno...» (II, 595),
Much of the humor of *Prometeo* resides in the abrupt contrasts between
the grandiose style of the classical epic and a lexicon which is thoroughly
plebeian and colloquial: [5] «Las grandes olas, llenas de ímpetu, empuja-
ban la balsa de un lado a otro... Ahora el Euros se la cedía a Zéfiros para
que éste la arrastrase, ahora el Notos se la cedía a Bóreas. Y la balsa se
hizo añicos» (II, 598-99). Modern man can no longer be a hero of mythical
proportions; our hero, our would-be Prometheus and self-styled Odysseus,
is in reality just another Juan Pérez — Juan Pérez Setignano, to be exact.
Because his name does not fit his ambitions, he has taken on the more
sonorous name of Marco de Setiñano. The contrast is evident here between
the ideal that he would like to be and the reality of his actual personality.

The novella starts out with a prologue rhapsody in the Homeric style.
The poem addresses someone (probably Marco although, by inference, all
men) asking why he insists on wandering over the earth looking for new
adventures when he will always carry with him his past life: «... llevas
contigo la vida pasada, / llevas el polvo de la jornada / en la sandalia
y en la vestidura» (II, 593). This person, loath to trust his own forces,
wanders down roads and pathways trod by others: «Jamás dejarás el
cayado.» As a result, he will always be a pilgrim and an exile: «Y te
sentirás desterrado en el fondo del corazón.» The poet's proposed solution
is to leave the dusty earth walked on by other men, and to trust his fortunes and fate to the sea: «No sigas rutas terrenales. / Gobierna sobre el
mar tu huida. / Echa pie en misteriosos arenales / cual si nacieses a una
nueva vida.» The implication seems to be that the sea is life and that
each person must make his own way:

> Sé tú mismo tu dueño, sé isleño.
> Haz de tu vida prodigioso sueño
> renovándose sin cesar.
> Abrázate al flotante leño.
> Echate a navegar por la mar.

The poem, a prologue to the whole novella, points out the lesson that
Marco fails to learn. The truth is that Marco never makes a real attempt
to be either Prometheus or Odysseus. Not trusting himself to the sea of
life, he is content to stay on land, hoping only to father the superman
since he can not be one himself.

The prose narrative relates, in a parody of the Homeric style, the
wanderings of a modern Odysseus who, when we meet him, is unhappily
trapped in the arms of a modern Kalypso whose real name is Federica
Gómez. He wants to leave but is apparently unable to confront her. Final-

---

[5] MARIANO BAQUERO GOYANES, *Perspectivismo y contraste. (De Cadalso a Pérez
de Ayala)* (Madrid: Editorial Gredos, 1963), p. 214.

ly he builds a raft and, one evening, sets out to sea. Thus the poem, in addition to serving as prologue to the entire novella, also foreshadows the events of the first chapter. It looks as if Marco will indeed try to find a new life for himself. He is shipwrecked and, at first, tries to embrace a «flotante leño» only to find that it does not serve him: «Odysseus cabalgó sobre uno de los troncos como sobre un caballo cerril, pero de nada le sirvió, y, a la postre, hubo de luchar a brazo contra las olas innumerables y rabiosas. Dábase por muerto, cuando el mar le escupió sobre un arenal» (II, 599). It is therefore with his own forces, and aided by life itself, that Odysseus will reach the land where he will meet his modern-day Nausikaá and start a new life.

The poem to the second chapter, entitled «Odysseus», tells of the king of Ithaca's long years in exile. In the prose narrative, we are given the real name of our modern Odysseus, and it explains his feelings of exile from his true home, ancient Greece: «Cuando leía la 'Odisea' derramaba lágrimas amargas, no de exaltación, sino de tristeza, como un desterrado en el tiempo que hubiera nacido con treinta siglos de retraso» (II, 602). Moreover, just as the king had been unrecognized on his return to Ithaca, so no one recognizes Juan Pérez, alias Marco de Setiñano, as an Odysseus in disguise: «El rey se tornó en un mendigo. / ¿Quién dirá que es el rey de antaño?» (II, 601). But the mythical Odysseus had a bow which only he could use and with which he could aim at the sky itself: «¿Llegará la flecha tan alto? / La flecha perdióse en el cielo.» The real Odysseus can reach where he aims, but not the modern Marco who does not even try: «Si alguno no apunta..., ¡menguado!» It seems likely that there is a play on words between *arco* and *arca*. Odysseus has an *arco* and Marco has an *arca*—that is, a sizable fortune which he inherits but does not use to reach the sky. He spends most of his time ruminating on where to aim. There is also the implication that he, in common with all men, has an *arca* of natural strengths that should be utilized to their fullest capacity:

> Tú, como yo, todos, hermano,
> todos somos como Odysseus,
> todos poseemos un arco,
> para los demás imposible,
> para uno mismo ágil y blando.

On the surface, Marco seems heroic because he is endowed with great physical beauty and strength. However, he lacks the spiritual component of *gracia*, as is shown in his retreat from amateur attempts at bullfighting:

> Halló muy presto que el arte de los toros no encerraba dificultades técnicas, ni exigía gran valor o habilidad. Su esencia era la gracia, don que los dioses otorgan a capricho, no la fuerza, cualidad que el hombre puede adquirir o robustecer. (II, 607)

Marco appreciates the necessity of joining *gracia* with *fuerza* and *astucia,* but in his own life Juan cultivates only the latter two: «Las más de las horas del día y de la noche se las pasaba sobre los libros. Y las horas de asueto las dedicaba a ejercitarse en actos gallardos y violentos: nadar, cabalgar» (II, 604). This is an excellent example of *mens sana in corpore sano,* an interest in harmonizing intellect with action. Since the integrating force of the spirit, *gracia,* is missing, Marco is unable to achieve his aspirations. Moreover, Marco does not really have a *mens sana.* He does everything to excess: not only does he read day and night (like Alonso Quijano) and engage in excessively strenuous exercise, but he is also much addicted to drink. Strangely enough, the various times that Pérez de Ayala mentions Marco's addiction, it is usually in connection with books, as in this example: «Contrajo otra vez el amor a los libros y se aplicó a poner en orden sus pensamientos y la moral de sus experiencias. En el amor a las libaciones ambrosianas no había desfallecido un punto» (II, 609). The impression is that both books and drink, and perhaps exercise, provide an escape from a confrontation with himself, from having to see that he is really quite an ordinary man:

> Escrutaba el futuro y todos los horizontes le parecían angostos para su ambición. Tenía el ánimo heroico y no sabía lo que quería; no sabía en qué resolverse... Quería ser él, él mismo, pero en forma que no acertaba todavía a definir... En suma, que sus anhelos eran tan vagos, que optó por esperar a que se fuesen concretando y esclareciendo. (II, 603)

Thus, instead of using his *arca* to aim for the sky, Marco simply lets time go by in the hope that he will eventually find some direction for his life. The fact is that Marco is an *abúlico.* He differs from Alberto in that he is physically more active and enjoys eating, drinking and lovemaking, but he is like Alberto in that he never is able to confront his true essence.

Since he himself cannot be Prometheus, Marco makes a calculated decision to be the father of Prometheus.[6] He realizes that

> la felicidad está reservada al hombre de acción; pero el hombre de acción no inventa la acción, la realiza; la acción la concibe el hombre de pensamiento; luego el hombre de pensamiento debe preceder al hombre de acción... (II, 610)

Marco («el hombre de pensamiento») will father Prometheus («el hombre de acción»). Again there is the dichotomy of the intellectual versus the life-force man, so important to the Generation of '98, which includes the dualism between spectator and actor that appears time and again in the works of Pérez de Ayala.

---

[6] MONROE Z. HAFTER, has discussed the possible influence of Galdós's Torquemada novels and Donald L. Fabian has studied the similarities between *Prometeo* and *Amor y pedagogía.* Torquemada, Avito Carrascal and Marco Setiñano are all similar in that they plan to engender prodigies.

Marco sets out on his project of fathering Prometheus conscious of his responsibilities, «con la clara conciencia de ser instrumento providencial y dilecto del genio de la especie» (II, 611). He is thirty-three years old, «en la plenitud de su edad» (II, 609). But this is a false *plenitud,* as Julio Matas has observed:

> Por otra parte, Marco pierde de vista una importante falla de su naturaleza individual. En varias ocasiones alude Ayala a su afición al alcohol... Marco aparece así a nuestros ojos como un hombre cuyas capacidades físicas van mermando, por efecto de una dilapidación de energías de la que él mismo no se da cuenta. Alcohol, concupiscencia, desorden vital, que viene a ser vaticinio del fracaso de una empresa para la que se necesita en principio, estar en la plenitud de las facultades corporales. [7]

The mythical Odysseus, although old, still had strength to pull his bow and aim his arrows at the sky and, even if he had not had the strength, he would have tried. Marco does not try, nor is he capable of engendering the proper strength in his son. This is what has become of the Odysseus legend in modern times.

The third chapter, called «Nausikaá», starts with a song to the natural man:

> Desnudo me parió mi madre,
> y hermoso, como un Inmortal.
> Yo soy dueño de mi destino.
> Ante mí, huye la adversidad.
> Yo soy el Hombre. Soy el Hombre,
> el Rey del mundo...
>
> (II, 613)

The sea has thrown him, nude, onto this stretch of land where he meets his Nausikaá with whom he will forge his immortality:

> Enlácenme tus blancos brazos,
> en el recio abrazo nupcial.
> Somos las hercúleas columnas
> donde el orbe apoyado está.
> En torno nuestro, cual guirnalda,
> se ha enroscado la eternidad.

In contrast to Marco and his impossible ambitions is the woman he chooses to marry, his modern Nausikaá whose real name is Perpetua Meana. Marco considers her first name very significant, and her last repugnant. Nausikaá is the first of many characters in Ayala's works who is a composite of male and female traits:

---

[7] JULIO MATAS, *Contra el honor (Las novelas normativas de Ramón Pérez de Ayala)* (Madrid: Seminarios y Ediciones, 1974), pp. 44-45.

> Era la esencia de la feminidad por su lindeza y su delicada frescura de rosa; un poco varonil por el carácter y la expresión... Dígase de paso que Perpetua nunca había gozado gran favor entre el mocerío masculino, sin duda por cierto aire de majestad e imperio que los galanes le reprochaban como poco femenino, un sí era no era hombruno. (II, 613-14)

Such mixtures of sexual stereotypes will be dealt with at greater length in subsequent chapters, but it should be pointed out that Pérez de Ayala is entirely in sympathy with Perpetua; he seems to feel that the perfect human is the one who has both male and female traits, perhaps because such a combination provides a better perspective on reality. There is no doubt that Perpetua has both feet on the ground. This is exemplified by her first meeting with Marco. When a friend screams that there is a nude man hiding behind a bush, all the damsels flee: «Solo Nausikaá permaneció, porque su corazón era fuerte y audaz, y adivinaba algún infortunio» (II, 600). Not only does she understand immediately that a disaster has taken place, she also has the heroic qualities that Marco lacks — «su corazón era fuerte y audaz». Later when she is pregnant, she is in contact with the sacredness of life:

> Sentía ella en sus entrañas, colmadas de ventura, la trepidación de la grande vida venidera, y él también creía sentir el armonioso bullicio de los gérmenes, comunicado a través de las dulces y laboriosas manos conyugales. (II, 630)

She seems to know that the new life in her womb is *ventura,* which means both happiness and danger, and that one enters life with trembling, whereas Marco has reduced the mystery of life to a positivistic union of cells. If the cells are perfect (and he has made every effort that this be so), then one can assume the perfection of the new life. His relation to Perpetua is quite similar to that between Avito Carrascal and Marina. Avito («La Forma») conceives of the universe in purely scientific terms, whereas Unamuno implies that Marina («la Materia») is actually more knowledgeable about life's secrets than he.

Chapter Four describes the courtship of Marco and Perpetua (in this chapter they are given their real names) and starts with a poem praising the strength and beauty of the young human body: «¡Cantemos la hermosura de la vida / corporal! En el cuerpo se concentra / toda la vida» (II, 616). The whole world waits joyously for «el gozoso ayuntamiento / de mujer y varón». By way of contrast to the beautiful young bodies of Marco and Perpetua, there are, in the prose narrative, two old bodies — that of the *marquesa* who, with the aid of paint pots and curling irons, resolutely attempts to give the impression of youth, and Perpetua's father, don Tesifonte, who is not at all pleased with the *marquesa*'s greeting: «—Le encuentro a usted decaído, muy avejentado» (II, 623). Neither of these two older people is willing to admit his age or to forego the pleasures of youth. As a result, their behavior renders them absurd: «Estaba la marquesa entregada a las artes cosméticas, en manos de una sirviente que le peinaba con prolijidad y artificio, de manera que la rala pelambre simulase la lozanía cabelluda de una res merina» (II, 616). As for don Tesifonte, «era extremeño, y, sin duda, descendía de casta de conquistadores porque las horas que no estaba en la oficina las dedicaba, exclusivamente, a la conquista de las criadas de servir» (II, 614).

The *marquesa* and don Tesifonte form a contrast to Perpetua and Marco: «Perpetua era una buena moza, bien repartida de carnes, pero sobria de curvas, conforme al canon griego; muy rubia y muy blanca, con la piel cubierta de vello plateado; los ojos, negros» (II, 613). Perpetua's reaction to Marco when she sees him for the first time is a purely sexual response: «Cuando le vi a usted..., lo primero pensé: ¡Qué guapo es este hombre! Era la primera vez que mi pensamiento deletreaba la palabra 'hombre'» (II, 627). Moreover, she has seen him first nude, then wrapped in a sheet, then wearing the clothes of a laborer and finally dressed as a gentleman. As Marco points out to her, this is the exact opposite of the normal procedure in a courtship:

> Gradualmente, conforme la intimidad y confianza se van estrechando, es posible que llegue a ver a su novio en mangas de camisa, con sábanas de baño... Lo que es seguro es que no le verá como usted me vio, hasta tanto que no se hayan casado ya. (II, 625)

Her response to him in his «natural state» makes them one with nature as described in the opening poem: «Naturaleza, / sin el deseo de dos cuerpos mozos, / es caótica, sorda, muda y ciega. / ¡Oh voluptuosidad de los sentidos! / ¡Oh cuerpo humano, templo de Belleza!» (II, 616).

The male and the female thus unite to bring forth the child prodigy. The fifth chapter, carrying the title «Prometeo», repeats the last line of the poem which precedes chapter four, but then goes on to imply that everything has gone wrong:

> ¡Oh cuerpo humano, templo de Belleza!
> Pobre templo de paganía.
> La lámpara del espíritu
> estaba sin óleo y sin vida.
> Pasó la juventud del templo.
> Se ha derrumbado en negras ruinas.

> (II, 629)

Marco has tried to insure that his son will be born perfect, but the child is deformed. Marco, believing in the perfection of science and unable to accept the imperfections of life, is undone by this dualism between reason and life. Perpetua, on the other hand, is like Fina in that she embodies a mother's loving acceptance not only of her son, whom she orders Marco to kiss, but also of her husband who becomes another child to her:

> Medio loco de dolor, Marco impuso sus labios en aquella carne triste y miserable, cuajada de tantos ensueños heroicos. Acercóse luego al lecho de Perpetua, dejó caer las rodillas en tierra y la cabeza sobre la almohada, y allí, junto a la dulce cara febril, color de cera, traslúcida por el misterio de la maternidad, lloró sin consuelo, sin ser dueño de sí, como un niño. (II, 631)

Again we should make a comparison between this novella and the ending of *Amor y pedagogía* where Marina calls her husband «¡Hijo mío!» and Avito calls her «¡Madre!». For Unamuno, a wife's love for her husband is often quite maternal, and the constantly changing roles of parent / spouse / child will be important in Ayala's later novels.

By the time he wrote *Prometeo*, Pérez de Ayala himself was married and had a son. His marriage seems to have been a happy one, and he had the reputation of being a loving father and grandfather. When his oldest son died in 1954, for example, he returned to Spain from Argentina in order to be a father to his grandchildren. There is an indication in *Prometeo* that the author had at last felt the integrating power of love. Alberto seems never to have really fallen in love with Fina, nor does Marco completely love Perpetua; in both cases, the love tends to be cerebral, as is Avito Carrascal's love for Marina. Perpetua seems to sense this lack because when Marco proposes marriage, she answers «yes» but with reservations: «—Una cosa quiero que me aclares, Marco. Has hablado antes del matrimonio como si se tratase de la cría de caballos, perros o cerdos de casta. Si no es más que eso..., no quiero casarme» (II, 627). Marco's reaction is, «—Eso debe ser; pero, además es el amor». His lack of complete surrender to love is the only thing that can explain his psychological destruction when Prometeo is born. Love, as the myth of Eros and Psyche reveals, should be felt only in the dark of the soul; it should never be brought out to the light to be analyzed. The difference between Alberto and Marco can be explained by the fact that when Pérez de Ayala wrote the tetralogy, he only intuited the healing power of love, not yet seeing clearly that the lack of love caused Alberto's disintegration. In *Prometeo,* although Marco also finally collapses, Pérez de Ayala is more consciously aware that love, not reason, would have saved him and, in the Tigre Juan novels, his message is that love, not bound by reason or the laws of society, is the only way to integrate the psyche.

While the first part of the introductory poem to chapter five foretells the downfall of the beautiful human body, exemplified by Marco and Perpetua, into the deformed body of the child Prometeo, the second part reintroduces the theme of Odysseus. This Odysseus is obviously Marco to whom the poetic message is directed:

A lo lejos, pasa Odysseus,
rugiendo de dolor y de ira.
El arco lleva a la espalda.
El arco de sus fechorías.

(II, 629)

There is a play on words between *arco* and *arca*. Marco's «'arca' de fe-chorías» would be his mistaken attitudes about engendering the super-man, his lack of real love for Perpetua, his excesses in drink and women as a younger man and, most of all, his lack of commitment. He himself should have tried to be the superman; he should not have demanded it of his son:

Odysseus, hombre esforzado,
que has puesto tan alto la mira
y has disparado tu flecha
contra el cielo que a todos cobija;
si otra vez repites la hazaña,
cuida de poner bien prendida
en la punta de la flecha tu alma,
tu propia alma dolorida,
y, con tu voluntad robusta,
luego, volando, al cielo envíala.

(II, 629)

Marco instinctively understands that he should have tested his own «alma dolorida» and that he sinned against nature. Although he is too abulic to figure out why, he feels guilt about having brought the boy into the world: «Marco traducía la expresión de su hijo en estos términos: ¿Por qué me has traído al mundo?» (II, 632). That may explain why there is no second attempt to create Prometheus. One has the impression that there were no more children in that marriage. [8]

When Marco first writes to his uncle of his decision to father the modern Prometheus, he describes Prometheus as an «hombre semidivino, redentor —que ahora más que nunca necesita de él la Humanidad— su-tura viva e intersección del cielo con la tierra» (II, 610). But this Pro-meteo is no «redentor». He is «un espíritu maléfico» and, in the final scene, when the milkmaid whom he accosts sees him, her reaction is to cross herself and say, «—¡Arreniego: *ye* el diaño!» (II, 634). Within the same person, then, is found the polar relationship between the Redeemer and the Devil.

In summary the dualistic elements in *Prometeo* are the following: 1) the use of poetry and prose, the one to synthesize and the other to

[8] ERNEST A. JOHNSON has pointed out the ironic contrast between Marco's frustrated «querer ser» and his son's successful «querer no ser». See his article, «So-bre 'Prometeo' de Pérez de Ayala», *Insula*, Nos. 100-101 (April-May 1954), p. 13.

analyze; 2) the use of the poem prefaces as an impassive Greek chorus which functions as spectator to the prose drama; 3) the very human Odysseus versus the semidivine Prometheus; 4) epic style together with colloquial lexicon; 5) the mythical Odysseus versus his modern counterpart; 6) the *abúlico* spectator of life versus the *hombre de acción*; 7) the beautiful but empty body versus the spirit; 8) woman and her natural love versus man and his cerebral love; and, finally, 9) the Redeemer versus the Devil.

There are some lesser examples of contrasting elements in this novella as, for example, the description of the sky as a ceiling for mankind but a floor for the gods; the fact that upon the birth of Prometeo, a bell tolls for the dead; and the comic touch that Lolita «la de la Carne» is really quite thin and has this nickname only «por haber nacido en la Puerta de la Carne». Another comic moment comes in a scene which presents the type of humor Pérez de Ayala will repeat frequently in his later works, particularly in *Belarmino y Apolonio*. When Perpetua comes to inform the *marquesa* of Marco's shipwreck, she enters the room saying:

> —Verá usted. Ocurre algo grave.
> La marquesa hubiera deseado componer una actitud estatuaria de patricia ecuanimidad, indicando que estaba dispuesta a recibir las nuevas más trágicas; pero la peinadora la tenía condenada a una postura ridícula e inmueble. (II, 617)

Pérez de Ayala seems to delight in showing that the sublime is almost always mixed with the ridiculous.

«LUZ DE DOMINGO»

The next story in the trilogy, however, includes very little that is comic. Although the novels of the tetralogy tend to melancholy and pessimism, it is a pessimism tinged with irony. *Luz de domingo* is a bitter and somber novel also, but without irony to lessen its full impact. The tale of Cástor and Balbina is truly pathetic.

Dinko Cvitanovic has made an excellent analysis of *Luz de domingo* from the point of view of medieval allegory. In his study, he makes a distinction between allegory and symbolism:

> En resumen..., me limitaré a indicar la que considero diferencia más evidente entre símbolo y alegoría: mientras el primero es multívoco, es decir incita a un orbe variado de interpretaciones, la alegoría es unívoca, es decir básicamente analógica e identificatoria. [9]

[9] DINKO CVITANOVIC, «Consideraciones sobre la mentalidad alegórica en *Luz de domingo*», in *Simposio Internacional Ramón Pérez de Ayala, 1880-1980*, ed. PELAYO H. FERNÁNDEZ (Gijón: Imprenta Flores, 1981), p. 54.

In his view, allegory contains dualism rather than perspectivism because it draws clear distinctions between good and evil. There is no polarity in this novella; the contrasts are obvious and dualistic. The Becerriles and the Chorizos are completely bad; Cástor and Balbina are perfectly good. This is one of the few times that Ayala categorizes. He seems to be going against his usual practice of giving multidimensional facets to any character or situation and, for this reason, I agree with Cvitanovic's interpretation of the story as medieval allegory. Some allegorical/dualistic elements he finds in the novella are the following:

First, the title of the novella: Cástor finds Sunday's sunlight «patética» and the light of the other days of the week «apática»:

> La luz del domingo es una luz que colma el espíritu, que le infunde vida, que realmente le hace *vivir* en un sentido profundo de experiencia espiritual que recuerda el *padecer* de Unamuno. Pero... debe recordarse aquí que la luz representa alegóricamente la precisa identificación con el espíritu... En una palabra, luz equivale a una síntesis de totalidad espiritual. [10]

Cvitanovic further notes that Sunday is a day of rest whereas the others are workdays, and that work «implica un estado de guerra, mientras el descanso trae la paz y la unión del hombre con la naturaleza». I agree that Sunday does indeed imply man's spiritual side, but I would add that the weekdays imply not only battle but also the materialistic side of man's nature. Certainly most of the wars of the world have been fought for materialistic reasons. In an allegorical interpretation of this novella, Cástor represents the spirit as opposed to the materialism of the Becerriles.

That the Becerriles represent the material world seems obvious to Cvitanovic:

> Los violadores de Balbina pertenecen al bando de los Becerriles, nombre sobre el cual no es necesario indagar demasiado..., pues adorar al becerro de oro significa rendir culto servil a las riquezas, a lo material y... a lo que... podemos llamar todo un catálogo de vicios. [11]

Granted that the Becerriles conjure up the image of the «becerro de oro» and the Canaanite religion as opposed to Judaism, in the same way the Chorizos —along with the phallic implications of that name— conjure up the pagan religions as opposed to Christianity. The Becerriles and the Chorizos thus represent the primitive pagan religions in opposition to Cástor and Balbina who represent the best in the Judeo-Christian tradition.

Cástor, in fact, is a symbol for Christ himself. He lets himself be taken by the Becerriles in a submissive manner that is reminiscent of Christ at Gethsemane. They tie him to a tree and proceed to «crucify» him by for-

[10] CVITANOVIC, p. 56.
[11] CVITANOVIC, p. 58.

cing the helpless lover to observe the rape of his fiancée. When Doro adds insult to injury by painting his nose and cheeks red like a clown, Cástor's reaction is again similar to that of Christ on the cross: «—¡Infame!... ¡Dios te perdone...!» (II, 658).

Cvitanovic also mentions the relationship between the name «Cástor» and the animal «castor», noting that the beaver «en los bestiarios es uno de los numerosos emblemas de la castidad...».[12] But it seems, rather, that the name Cástor is important because of its association with Pollux and the fact that the myth of these twin brothers deals with the dualism of mortality versus divinity. According to the myth, these brothers were the sons of Leda and different fathers; Pollux was divine because his father was Zeus, whereas Castor the son of King Tyndareus of Sparta, was mortal. «Nevertheless, both brothers, Castor and Pollux, were often called 'sons of Zeus'; indeed, the Greek name they are best known by, the *Dioscouri,* means 'the striplings of Zeus'. On the other hand, they were also called 'sons of Tyndareus', the *Tyndaridae*».[13] Since the mortal Castor is always associated with his divine twin and because one cannot be considered without the other, both become both divine and mortal. When Castor is killed in a dispute about oxen (the Becerriles come to mind), Zeus in pity allows the inconsolable Pollux to share eternity with his brother so that «the two were never separated again. One day they dwelt in Hades, the next in Olympus, always together».[14] Thus, Cástor is Christlike not only in his behavior, but also because he represents a mythical hero who was son of god and son of man. He embodies the mortality/divinity dualism by the immediate association that is made between him and his twin brother Pollux.

Just as the prose narrative of *Luz de domingo* is fashioned on the medieval allegory, the poems that precede each chapter also follow the medieval *romances*. The poem that precedes the first chapter makes a contrast between the sweetness of a humble but happy home as opposed to the palace of the king:

> Mi cabezal está lleno—de fina hierba aromada;
> lleno de tiernas memorias—e ilusiones del mañana.
> El rey en su cabezal—se reclina y no descansa,
> que le acosan mil cuidados—y mil temores le asaltan.
> ¡Cuántas noches, con mi amor—soñé que me desposaba!...
> ¡Rincón de mis días felices!—¡Mi casa, mi dulce casa!
> Si no fuera por casarme,—cierto que nunca os dejara.

> (II, 639)

---

[12] CVITANOVIC, p. 57.

[13] EDITH HAMILTON, *Mythology* (New York: The New American Library, 1942), p. 41.

[14] EDITH HAMILTON, p. 42.

In this chapter, Cástor is thinking with melancholy that he will soon be leaving this house in which he has lived for more than a year. Orphaned as a child, this is the first home he has ever known and doña Predestinación has been like a mother to him. [15] The irony is that this house is a *casa de huéspedes,* the first of several which will appear in the works of Ayala. [16] Whereas ordinarily one is lonely in a boarding house, for Castor this has been a real home.

Chapter two starts with a poem which reveals the happiness in Cástor's heart. It is Sunday and the last banns will be proclaimed for him and Balbina. They plan to marry the following Friday:

> La campana de la iglesia —a ti y a mí nos llamó.
> ¡Cuál repica la campana —dentro de mi corazón!
> Con mi mocina, a la iglesia, —a tomar los dichos voy.
> ¡Mañanas de abril y mayo, —galanas y con amor!

(II, 643)

But at the end of the poem, there is a sinister word of warning: «La mala culebra / dejó oír su voz. / Durmió durante el invierno, / despertóla la calor.» Cástor had planned to go to church with Balbina, but he suddenly remembers that the Ayuntamiento will meet that morning and he, as secretary, is obliged to attend. The town is in the power of a decadent family of aristocrats, the Becerriles, and the mayor holds a grudge against Balbina's grandfather, don Joaco, who will not sell him a piece of land. Doña Predestinación suspects that the mayor has called the session for that particular Sunday when the last banns will be announced with the intention of annoying Cástor. She warns Cástor that the Becerriles plan some sort of revenge because, in addition to the mayor's hostility, three of his sons had unsuccessfully courted Balbina and, therefore, they also hold grudges against the young lovers. But the good-natured Cástor cannot believe that anyone wishes to harm him:

> En su alma no habían penetrado las inquietudes y sobresaltos de doña Predestinación...
> Salió Cástor camino de la iglesia. Apenas puso el pie en la calle, había olvidado enteramente los advertimientos, prevenciones y cuidados de doña Predestinación. (II, 646)

---

[15] VICENTE RANGEL feels that doña Predestinación's «maternal» attitude toward Cástor is, in reality, a sublimated sexual attraction. See his article, «Las novelas poemáticas de Ramón Pérez de Ayala: una interpretación estilística de *Luz de domingo*», *Explicación de Textos Literarios,* 7, ii (1978-79), 201-02.

[16] In *Belarmino y Apolonio,* Pérez de Ayala will make a detailed examination of the place of the *casa de huéspedes* in Spanish society. The subject seems to intrigue him.

The poem to chapter three laments the decadence of the modern-day nobility:

Caballeros hidalgotes—aposentan en palacios.
Sobre el dintel de la puerta—tienen escudos labrados;
cobijo para los canes,—cuadra para los caballos.
Vino y yantar en la mesa—están siempre aparejados.
A falta de hacienda propia,—la quitan a los villanos.
Por señores absolutos—ha tiempo se han titulado.
Derrocaban los molinos,—robaban harina y grano,
prendían los molineros.—Por doquiera hacen estrago.
Ponen las mozas encinta,—cuernos a los maridados.
No hay hembra con que no yazgan,—por fuerza si no es de grado.
¡Ved la flor de la hidalguía—y la nobleza de antaño!

(II, 647)

The prose narrative of chapter three describes the political situation of Cenciella in the hands of the Becerriles and the Chorizos. The Chorizos are the bourgeoisie and the Becerriles are the aristocracy. As the poem suggests, that aristocracy has lost all traces of true nobility:

Los Becerriles no tenían fuerza propia. Eran simplemente rústico instrumento de los gobernantes y los poderosos, residentes en la capital de la provincia y en Madrid. Constituían una vasta familia. Todos ellos ostentaban escudo en sus casas. No trabajaban, ni hacían cosa de provecho. Eran grandes cazadores, tahúres, borrachines y querellosos. Cometían con impunidad todo linaje de desafueros. Durante muchos años habían sido los tiranos del pueblo. (II, 648-49)

Nicolás «el Perinolo», head of the Chorizos, tries to convince Cástor to make an open declaration in favor of the plebeian party, but Cástor refuses to take sides. As a result, he incurs the suspicion of both parties and, in this atmosphere of hostility (of which he is unaware), the Ayuntamiento starts its meeting to determine the yearly tax assessment.

The poem which precedes chapter four describes a nightmare in which seven Becerriles which is narrated in this chapter. The relationship be-refuge in the heart of the poet:

Síguenla los siete halcones.—Por mi pecho éntranse ya,
El pecho me han quebrantado.—Sobre la cuitada dan.
Con sus garras la desgarran,—y a mi corazón igual.
¡Cuánta sangre! ¡Cuánta sangre!—No cesa de borbotar.
La sangre de ella y la mía—se han revuelto en un caudal.
Hay sueños que quedan sueños—y otros que salen verdad.

(II, 651)

The poem records in metaphorical language the rape of Balbina by the seven Becerriles which is narrated in this chapter. The relationship between poetry and prose of the *novelas poemáticas* is here reversed. Usually the poetry functions as the impassive spectator to the prose drama, but

55

in this chapter the pathos is found in the poem, while the prose narrative describes the rape with cold detachment: «Y uno tras de otro, los siete fueron infamando a Balbina a la faz de Cástor. La muchacha había perdido el sentido» (II, 657).

Justice is the subject of the poem that begins chapter five:

> Hasta la silla del rey—llega de gente un gran golpe.
> Por todos habla un buen viejo.—Estas fueron sus razones.
> Justicia pedimos, rey,—en los siete forzadores,
> que rey que no hace justicia—no debe vivir en Corte...
>
> (II, 660)

But no justice can be had from the king:

> El rey respondiera: «Vedme—el más triste de los hombres,
> que la corona no es mía—y vivo como en prisiones.
> Ellos mandan en el reino,—los malos gobernadores.
> Vosotros, fieles vasallos,—afilad presto las hoces
> y haced cumplida cosecha—de cabezas de traidores.»

In the narrative the «buen viejo» of the poem is don Joaco who wants to take the law into his own hands. When Cástor implies that he is leaving the punishment of the Becerriles to God («¿No habrá justicia en el cielo?»), Joaco replies: «—El cielo está muy alto. En sus cosas no debemos meternos nosotros, que vivimos acá abajo. Acá abajo ya es sabido que no hay más justicia que la que uno se toma por su mano. Yo ya los hubiera matado a todos ellos...» (II, 661). Since he realizes that killing all seven Becerriles is impossible, he decides to bring a suit for damages against them, but Cástor is opposed to this idea because he does not want Balbina to undergo the public humiliation of the trial. The conclusion is that no justice can be had for this affront. Times have changed since the days of the Cid, and one now understands the two lines from the *Poema de Myo Cid* which introduce *Luz de domingo*: «¡Quál ventura serie esta, si ploguiese al Creador, / que assomasse essora el Cid Campeador!» (II, 638).

Chapter six tells of the inevitable gossip and the suffering of Balbina and Cástor, made worse by the discovery that she is pregnant:

> «Vasija quebrada y rota—nunca de agua se llenó.
> Rosa pisada de zuecos—es tierra que ya no es flor.
> . . . .
> La doncella con mancilla—no es doncella, vive Dios.
> Aunque le sierren los cuernos,—el cabrón sigue cabrón.»
> Por las puertas de las casas,—con ronca y sonante voz,
> así iba cantando un ciego,—cazurro, viejo y burlón.
> La niña que lo escuchaba—desfallecía de dolor.
> El amante la besaba,—con llanto en el corazón;
> que la niña estaba encinta.—¿Encinta de un forzador?
>
> (II, 664)

Balbina, Cástor and the grandfather fear that the child may not be Cástor's. The mayor of Cenciella, realizing that the rape of Balbina could be used by the Chorizos against the Becerriles, has Cástor transferred to Pilares, but even there the malicious gossip follows:

> En el periódico, un literato provinciano refería la afrenta de la pomarada de la ermita no a la manera castellana del *Poema del Cid,* sino contrahaciendo el estilo irónico y lascivo de Boccaccio. Y la nueva de la afrenta cundió hasta el barrio en donde Cástor y Balbina vivían. (II, 665)

The child is born in Pilares and Cástor, in an effort to get as far away as possible from Cenciella, seeks and obtains a post in Tejeros. During the last-minute preparations for the move, Cástor, helping Balbina swaddle the child, discovers a birthmark on the boy's body similar to one on his own. The child is his own son, after all.

Chapter seven shows the family going south in search of the limpid Castilian sunlight. This is one of the few times in Pérez de Ayala's novels that the strong sun and heat of the south seem preferable to the mists of the north:

> Dejaron las tierras grises,—en donde el sol nunca sale;
> la neblina insinuativa,—que finge ensueños falaces.
> No vuelven atrás el rostro.—Huyen, huyen anhelantes,
> y el fantasma del recuerdo—les persigue, a los alcances.
> Salen a la ancha Castilla—por el puerto de Pinares.
> La tierra es púrpura y oro,—de amapolas y trigales.
> Ancha es Castilla. Su cielo—es de seda azul joyante.
> No hay fantasmas. No hay neblina.—Todo es puro, claro y grave.
> Un sol de justicia alumbra—las hazas de ocre y de almagre.
>
> (II, 667)

Cástor and Balbina, don Joaco and the baby have been living in Tejeros for more than a year. Cástor considers that they are finally happy and even Balbina is now able to talk about the past with more equanimity. But unfortunately the gossip follows them, even to Tejeros. Their neighbors, who have come to love them, cannot understand why the Becerriles were not hanged for their crime. The spread of the gossip from the north and the neighbors' sentiments are metaphorically described in the last lines of the introductory poem:

> Sol de justicia. ¡A Dios plegue—que no sople el cierzo infame
> y las cosechas malogre,—y traiga consigo el hambre!
>
> ¡Hambre de justicia!
> Hambre negra
> Hambre insaciable.

In a final desperate attempt to escape, the grandfather decides to sell his property and take the family to America where, he believes, they can live happily under constant sunshine.

The poem which prefaces the last chapter has two parts. In the first, the poet condemns a society which allows itself to be victimized by corrupt political bosses:

> Pobre Castilla la llana,—que no puede ver el mar.
> Pobre terruñero, adscrito—a la gleba de un erial.
> Con quebranto, de vosotros—me parto. Con Dios quedad.
> Pueblo sobrio, pueblo hidalgo,—prez de hidalguía cabal;
> triste de ti, que la infamia—llegó a meterse en tu hogar.
> . . . .
> Maldito de Dios el pueblo—que se deja amiseriar,
> que humilla su cuello al yugo—y moja en llanto su pan.
> Mal haya aquel que, cobarde,—se deja mal gobernar.
> Quédense los regidores—solos, un tal para un cual.
>
> (II, 670)

In the prose narrative one discovers that the Becerriles have lost their political power in Cenciella and the Chorizos are now in control. The situation, however, has gone from bad to worse. On the ship that is taking them to America, Cástor discovers that he is traveling with some acquaintances from Cenciella. He has been trying to flee from their gossip and sees now that this will be impossible, and they are attempting to escape the political corruption of provincial Spain: «—Salimos huidos del pueblo. Allí no se puede vivir. Ya ve usted que cuando los Becerriles aquello iba mal. Bien lo sabe usted y la pobre Balbina. Pues con los Chorizos, mucho peor» (II, 672).

The second part of the poem foreshadows the end of the story. It describes the ship's setting sail for the New World and finishes with the line: «Salió mas adentro el buque, —con rumbo a la Eternidad.» The ship is wrecked by a storm and

> Cástor y Balbina se dejaron morir dulcemente, abrazados el uno al otro, como un solo cuerpo. Y así, confundidas las dos almas en un aliento, volaron al país de la Suma Concordia, en donde no existen Becerriles ni Chorizos, y brilla eternamente la pura e increada luz dominical. (II, 672)

In addition to the poetry/prose dualism and the good/bad dualism of the allegory, there occur other contrasts in this novella that have appeared before in the works of Pérez de Ayala. For example, the theme of art versus life. When Cástor paints a picture on that idyllic Sunday afternoon, he asks Balbina's opinion and she answers, «—A mí me gusta más que las cosas de verdad de donde lo has tomado» (II, 654).

Dualism within the same person is shown by conflicting emotions. For example, when doña Predestinación tells Cástor that don Joaco has accepted him as Balbina's fiancé, she weeps and smiles at the same time. Then, when the child is born, both Cástor and the grandfather experience contradictory feelings. Not knowing whether he is the father, «Cástor sufría más que nunca. Quería querer al niño y se le figuraba que no podía hacerlo. No quería quererlo, y se le figuraba que lo quería, a pesar suyo» (II, 666). And the grandfather at first wants to kill the newborn child, but later, «se encariñó en seguida con el mamoncillo; y de seco y áspero que era se trocó en empalagoso, sobón y sensiblero» (II, 666). It is significant that the old man and the child are the only ones to survive the shipwreck—one approaching death, the other just beginning life. Finally, we have the dualism of sexual ambivalence—that is, one person taking on the characteristics of the opposite sex. On the night the newlyweds return to Cenciella from their honeymoon, a group of merrymakers create a derisive din outside the house and doña Predestinación, «usurpando el papel de campeón que hubiera correspondido mejor a un hombre», [17] drives them away.

«LA CAÍDA DE LOS LIMONES»

Luz de domingo ends with Cástor and Balbina trying to escape to America. On the boat they meet people from their home town who are fleeing from the political bosses who have been making life in Cenciella impossible for everybody. Whether power is with the Becerriles or Chorizos, the problem of unrestrained authority remains the same.

In *La caída de los Limones,* the last novella of this trilogy, the aristocratic forces unite with the plebeian in the marriage of Fernanda Uceda of the ancient city of Guadalfranco to Enrique Limón, a newcomer of unknown origin. As Francisco Agustín has pointed out, it is the union of two contrasting elements: «el Poder hereditario, pasivo..., con el advenedizo y activo...». [18] This union still does not bring moderation; the greed for power corrupts and excessive authority brings about its own downfall. The novel is basically an analysis of power and its subsequent decline, but it also deals with such other dualistic elements as aristocrats and plebeians, past and present, life and death, day and night, light and darkness. The predominant element is a chiaroscuro contrast of light and dark.

The poem that introduces the first chapter deals with a classical *ubi sunt* theme: two roses that were once young, fresh, and beautiful are now «dos pobres rosas secas, / de carne marchita y morena». The thorns that

[17] RANGEL, p. 202.
[18] FRANCISCO AGUSTÍN, *Ramón Pérez de Ayala. Su vida y obras* (Madrid: Imprenta de G. Hernández y Galo Sáez, 1927), p. 168.

had once been «adorno y para defensa» are now thrust into their own hearts «como duras flechas». The dualistic opposition between a past of youth, beauty, and pride, versus a withered and downtrodden present is evident here. The last line of the poem bewails this contrast: «¡En qué paró tanta lindeza!» (II, 675).

The prose introduces a first-person narrator who is describing the atmosphere of a typical *casa de huéspedes* in Madrid. One quickly recognizes an element that appears later in *Belarmino y Apolonio*: the democratic aspect of Spanish boarding houses. The guests have their meals at a round table which, ever since King Arthur, has been taken to mean that everyone seated there is equal. The table thus serves as a unifying force for such disparate elements as «el jefe del partido republicano de Tarazona» who sits there together with the «canónigo de Atocha», and the two aristocratic ladies who arouse the curiosity of the narrator, an obscure law student. Since the circle is a symbol for wholeness, it seems that this is a first attempt by our author to bring dualistic elements together into a polaristic relationship.

One of the outstanding characteristics of a typical *casa de huéspedes* is the happy chatter and familiarity by which newcomers are soon integrated into the group, and everybody knows everybody else's business almost immediately. The two aloof and silent women who enter the story form a stark contrast with this group:

> Las dos señoras enigmáticas aparecen en el ambiente costumbrista de la pensión. Está bien elegida la perspectiva (confianza, casi familiar, símbolo de su caída) para presentar a las dos aristócratas que... son las únicas no abiertas en ese ambiente tan abierto. Para mostrarlo, les dirigen la palabra dos tipos simbólicos del ambiente: el republicano y el cura. [19]

These ladies, of course, are the «dos pobres rosas secas» of the introductory poem. The narrator says that their age would be hard to calculate:

> Estaban entrambas dentro de ese dilatado lapso de tiempo que abarca desde el punto en que la mujer comienza a perder juventud, lozanía e incentivo, hasta el acabamiento de toda gracia de feminidad y hermosura, edad que va de los treinta, y aun menos, a los cincuenta, y aun más, desenvolviéndose con tan sutiles y personales gradaciones que es punto menos que imposible calcularles los años... (II, 677)

The author treats the two women as one entity, which they are to the other guests of the boarding house, although Dominica is thirteen years younger than Fernanda and is quite different in personality. The only differentiating characteristic noted by the narrator is the physical one of «el vello, sedeño y vaporoso en un rostro, se correspondía con el vello hirsuto y áspero del otro rostro» (II, 678). Thus, one is made aware

---

[19] AMORÓS, *La novela intelectual*, p. 275.

indirectly of Dominica's femininity as opposed to the masculine traits of her older sister.

The chapter ends with a stylistic bifurcation noted by Frances Weber. First, the author describes the women in delicate and erudite terms: «Eran humildemente dolorosas. Su dolor... sugería la idea de un destino mujeril malogrado, algo así como la tristeza de la virginidad vetusta», but, suddenly, the change of tone in the very next sentence reflects «the harsh terms of vulgar opinion»: [20] «O como se dice en el duro lenguaje de cada día, tenían toda la traza de ser dos solteronas» (II, 678).

The poem that introduces the second chapter opposes day, «el blanco caballero», and night, «el negro paladín». They chase each other in circles, but one never catches the other. The unifying circle symbolized by «el Angelus del alba» and «el Angelus vespertino» introduces in turn the idea of bells: «Talán. / Campana de plata. / Ha nacido un nuevo cristiano. / ¡Oh blanco misterio!» (II, 679). The contrast to this is: «Talán, talán. / Campana de bronce. / ¡Oh negro arcano! / Llevan un hombre al cementerio.» The opposition of day and night symbolizing birth and death is represented specifically by the colors white and black.

The previous chapter emphasized the «virginidad vetusta» of the two unknown ladies. In the second chapter, the young Mariquita, daughter of the owner of the boarding house, is awaiting «el primer fruto de bendición para antes de terminar el mes» (II, 679). The joyous fecundity of this young woman is a marked contrast to the austere sadness of the sisters. She represents life and they, death.

The first paragraph gives a description of the sewing room which at present is being utilized in preparation for the arrival of the child: «En el cuarto de coser, todo era laboriosidad, algazara y blancura preparando la canastilla para el crío» (II, 679). White is the predominant color in these preparations: «Lo único que turbaba el albo reposo eran ciertas disquisiciones polémicas sobre el sexo de la criatura» (II, 680). One afternoon, however, the narrator is startled to see swatches of black cloth among the white:

> Una tarde, al entrar en el cuarto de costura, hallé una novedad que me sobrecogió al pronto. Mezcladas con las piezas de lo blanco había algunas piezas negras de lana y satén. Las dos señoras desconocidas, acompañadas de una costurera, cortaban en las telas de luto. Doña Trina y Mariquita cosían con ardimiento los blancos atavíos sin reparar en el contraste. (II, 680)

Hence death is introduced in the midst of birth. Also, this death will occur *in the middle* of the day: «—Pues que antes del mediodía no estarán de luto, y desde el mediodía ya estarán de luto» (II, 681). Again the duality forms a circle of day and night and birth and death, everything

---

[20] WEBER, *The Literary Perspectivism of Ramón Pérez de Ayala*, p. 43.

equal, as it was with the round table. At this point, the two ladies are identified as «las señoritas de Limón, de los Limones de Guadalfranco» (II, 681).

A poem with several themes introduces chapter three. The first is an old city built of the contrasting elements of stone and mud: «Vieja ciudad de piedra cincelada / y de barro el más deleznable. / Eternidad eternizada / y vanidad de lo mudable» (II, 682). The prose narrative describes the once great city of Guadalfranco:

> Encerraba dentro de sus muros fuertes cuarenta mil casas con otros tantos vecinos... La agricultura florecía asombrosamente, merced a mil ingeniosos artificios con que los moriscos regaban y cultivaban la tierra, la cual era fecunda sobre todo en alcornoque. (II, 684-85)

In contrast to its past: «Hoy en día, Guadalfranco no cuenta arriba de veinte mil moradores... De la riqueza y esplendor antiguos no quedan sino los alcornoques» (II, 685). As Pelayo H. Fernández has remarked:

> Nuevo poema de facetas antitéticas enfrenta el ayer glorioso de la ciudad de Guadalfranco con el hoy decrépito. Los términos contradictorios piedra-barro, eternidad-mudable, sirven de meditación a modo de *leitmotif* del viejo *ubi sunt*. [21]

There is also a play on words with *alcornoque* which can mean «corktree» and as such represents the wealth of Guadalfranco, but it also has the slang meaning of «blockhead» or «stupid fellow», an apt description of all that is left in present-day Guadalfranco.

The republicans were responsible for the joke that Guadalfranco was an imaginary city invented by the national politician Sagasta in order to give his sycophantic favorites their reward. This imaginary Guadalfranco does not seem to be unusual: «¡Son tantas las ciudades españolas que parecen inventadas por Sagasta!... Ciudades que un tiempo fueron heroicas, esforzadas, activas y abundantes, hoy sólo tienen una existencia imaginaria y soporífera» (II, 684). This passage, reminiscent of Clarín's introduction to *La Regenta*, expresses the idea of the vanished glory of Spain so popular with the Generation of '98 and which was alluded to in the Antonio Machado style of the introductory poem: «Eternidad eternizada / y vanidad de lo mudable.»

The second point of the introductory poem is that of the perishing hidalgos:

> Dormir, morir. Nada más quiero.
> Apreté entre mis ávidas manos
> el haz fabuloso y rotundo
> que forman los mares livianos

---

[21] FERNÁNDEZ, *Estudios sobre Ramón Pérez de Ayala*, p. 115.

y las tierras firmes del mundo.
Y todo fue un fútil empeño
—dijo el hidalgo moribundo.

(II, 682)

In the prose narrative, the hidalgos are the Ucedas of Guadalfranco. At one time they were a great family with many privileges, but little by little their greatness diminished. The last three lines of the introductory poem obviously refer to Arias, the last of the Ucedas, who dreams of conquering empires like his glorious ancestor but whose grandiose dreams are halted by his *abulia,* another theme of the generation of '98: «Están posadas en su cabeza / la mariposa del ensueño / y el escorpión de la pereza.» The futile endeavors of the hidalgo are explained as quixotic dreams that came to naught because of a basic sloth or, as Arias will explain later, «he sido perezoso porque sabía que jamás llegaría a ejecutar acciones tan altas como yo anhelaba» (II, 717). In both the poetry and the prose, then, we have the opposition between a glorious past and a decadent present and, within the same person (Arias), the opposition between the desire to perform noble deeds and the lack of *voluntad* to carry them out.

The poem preceding chapter four describes a prince and his retinue in an enchanted garden. The style shows the influence of Rubén Darío:

El príncipe lindo pasea el jardín.
Al diestro, la reina, con gran capirote.
Detrás la nodriza conduce el mastín
vestida con túnica de verde anascote.

El señor Jilguero, trovero laureado,
canta mil lisonjas al príncipe real:
«El mundo es un vasto país encantado,
y tú eres del mundo señor natural.»

(II, 689)

In the final strophe, however, a somber *Mirlo,* serving as contrast to the gaily-colored *Jilguero,* exclaims with foreboding: «Señor, que nunca se rompa este encantamiento.» Thus one is again reminded of the unreal, dreamlike quality of the enchanted though precarious life in Guadalfranco.

The prose narrative of the fourth chapter portrays the family into which Arias was born. His mother died at his birth and his oldest sister, Fernanda, was left in charge of the household. However, Fernanda is more masculine than feminine. In fact, the author mixes genders in describing her birth: «Al primogénito, que fue niña...» (II, 687). Fernanda should have been a boy, the heir to the wealth and power of the family.

As her father's administrative assistant, she demonstrates a keen under-standing of political problems. Since she is not maternal, she solves the burden of taking care of the newly-born Arias by hiring a nurse and rele-gating the child, together with Dominica and Dominica's pet dog, to a back portion of the house under the care of an old servant. There they are later joined by Arias's «hermano de leche», Bermudo, and all three children grow up in this enchanted garden, completely separated from the reality of the outside world:

> Así transcurrieron algunos años. Siempre lo mismo. Arias, como un prínci-pe, hermoso y benigno. Dominica, la reina madre; madre, a la par que niña, por gracioso milagro. Bermudo, como el mastín del príncipe. Además, un gno-mo, velludo y riente. Luego, la vieja nodriza y un hada bondadosa y providen-te, revestida con el pergenio engañoso de criada vieja. Y más allá de aquel mundo quieto, el mundo de las disputas, de los tráfagos, presidido por la adus-ta Fernanda y el viejo papá, que muy de tarde en tarde caía por Guadalfranco, a visitar los estados y dar un beso a los hijos. (II, 691)

This prose account sketches the same world described in the *modernista* poem, and now one senses that the Mirlo's misgivings have some found-ation. Obviously, the real world will eventually invade this enchanted kingdom.

The poem to chapter five is a sharp reminder that all deeds, both good and bad, will be lost in time: «Las hazañas y los desmanes / se derriten en el olvido.» Also, it is a warning for guiding one's boat down the river of life: «¡Quiera Dios que no te remanses / sobre la presa del molino!» (II, 692). The poem synthesizes in metaphors what will occur.

The prose narrative describes the child Arias as «agraciado, sonriente, dulce y amable en su debilidad» (II, 690). His polaristic partner is his «hermano de leche», Bermudo, who is bursting with health but is somewhat stupid and awkward. Bermudo has difficulty expressing himself, whereas Arias is a spellbinding story-teller:

> Arias refería fantaseadas aventuras, con palabra inflamada y tan plástica que, por momentos, Dominica, con voz ronca, interrumpía murmurando:
> —¡Qué hermoso es lo que dices, Arias! ¡Y qué verdadero! Parece como si lo viese con mis ojos. (II, 692)

The whole chapter is a study of the dualism of the real versus the ideal. As the «novelas de caballería» influenced Don Quijote, so Arias inflames his listeners with stories from the *Conquista de Nueva España,* to the point that the children decide to sail on voyages of discovery to conquer «países para que los gobernasen su hermana Fernanda y el rey de España» (II, 693). That night they sail down the river in a small boat but, since they do not know how to guide the craft, they are caught in the mill dam where they are found the following day. This one attempt at action is cut short by their obvious lack of experience with reality; from now on they will have to be content with dreams: «Esta fue la primera y última aventura en acción. Las demás fueron aventuras de fantasía en la penumbra vespertina del huerto» (II, 694). Back they go to their enchanted garden.

The poem of chapter six recounts the tale of a little girl adored and praised by everybody. Only her doll Cordelia offers no word of praise. Because the doll is mute and will not say flattering things to her, the little girl, in a rage, shatters the doll on the floor and stamps on it, whereupon a miracle happens:

> Y habla entonces por un milagro,
> antes de morir, la muñeca:
> «Yo te quería más que nadie
> aunque decirlo no pudiera.»

(II, 695)

The prose of chapter six narrates the story of the only disagreement between Dominica and Arias. Dominica is very different from Fernanda:

> Dominica destaca por sus instintos maternales y, en cierto modo, sustituye a la madre en el corazón de Arias, al que adora y trata como a un muñequito que fuera su propio hijo. Las dos hermanas engendran una dicotomía, crean un contraste, un claroscuro. [22]

Dominica has indeed been a mother to Arias and is part of his Oedipus complex. His rival is not his father, who spends most of the time in Madrid and whom he rarely sees, but, rather, Dominica's pet dog, Delfín, referred to several times as the gnome of that enchanted world. Arias grows to hate Delfín and, in a moment of fury, hurls the dog against a wall, hurting it badly. The wounded animal, like the doll in the poem, seems to respond to this treatment only with love:

> Desde el sitio en donde yacía inmóvil, miraba a Arias con pupila resignada, amorosa y suplicante, como si le dijese: «No me importa morir. Estoy ya tan viejo... Soy una plepa. Pero ¿por qué te has ofendido conmigo? ¿Por qué me has maltratado siempre? ¿Por qué me has querido tan mal? Yo siempre te he querido, Arias, hermano de Dominica. Aún recuerdo cuando eras tan pequeño como yo, que no podías andar..., y yo te hacía reír, y tú jugabas conmigo...» (II, 697)

Arias is immediately overcome with remorse and begs Delfín's forgiveness. The dog recovers and in its last few months of life «fue casi más amigo de Arias que de Dominica».

Poem number seven extols Power and makes clear its ambivalent nature:

---

[22] FERNÁNDEZ, p. 120.

¡Poder! ¡Poder! ¡Oh vino de divina
borrachera! El más alto de los bienes.

. . . .

¡Mando! ¡Poder! ¡Oh monstruo que hasta el cielo
alzas, para robar una gavilla
de estrellas, tus dos brazos altaneros.
Y, sin embargo, son tus pies de arcilla.

(II, 699)

Chapter seven studies the power of the Limones. The adolescent Arias is isolated by the power of his family. He has no friends except the ever-faithful Bermudo:

> Bermudo, hermano de leche de Arias, es el vivo contraste de éste. Se había criado en el campo y «reventaba de salud, rusticidad y rubicundez» —el mismo nombre de pila que lleva le sienta a la perfección, pues en su etimología significa «que tiene ánimo de oso»—. Una lealtad y adhesión caninas —animaloides— distinguirán siempre su modo de ser y su conducta. De hecho, se ve inmediatamente que Ayala ha querido ofrecernos dos mitades que se complementan y aportan un valor simbólico al argumento. [23]

Followed by Bermudo, Arias roams the streets of Guadalfranco at night. He is attracted by the interiors of the houses wherein he can catch glimpses of light and warmth:

> Las ventanas de los pisos bajos estaban abiertas; las moradas, con luz. Se veían los interiores profundos; escenas de familia. Se oía rumoreo de charlas quedas, risas, voces de discordia, el llanto de un niño, un piano, una guitarra, una canción. (II, 699-700)

Arias is aware that the whole town is dependent on the will of his father and Fernanda, and that he will be inheriting that power in the not-too-distant future. But power, as the poem indicates, has «pies de arcilla». Arias is unaware that the power of the Limón family is already beginning to crumble:

> Pero don Arias, extraviado en la niebla de sus quimeras e imaginaciones, ignoraba que el feudo paternal se agrietaba y desmoronaba. La ciudad y la provincia aborrecían la opresión caciquil. (II, 700)

The introductory poem declares that for Power «los hombres venden a su propia madre / o dan en prenda el alma a Satanás». The prose narrative introduces a young man who has come to court Dominica, but one suspects that what attracts him is her family's wealth and power:

> Próspero Merlo, joven abogado de altaneras miras, inteligencia despejada y lengua fluida, comenzó a visitar con asiduidad la casa de los Limones. Afiliose,

[23] FERNÁNDEZ, pp. 120-21.

desde luego, en el partido, por la cuenta que le tenía, y fue en la ciudad y en la comarca el más elocuente y fervoroso vocero de la causa caciquil. Probaba a quien quería oírle lo paternal, saludable y suculento del régimen de cacicato. (II, 700-01)

The entrance of Merlo into the family scene brings to mind the forebodings of the *Mirlo* in the poem to chapter four.

The last two lines of the poem show the duality of Power itself: «¡Poder causar al enemigo un daño...! / ¡Poder brindar al allegado un bien...!» Arias, insanely jealous of his sister's suitor, flies into a rage and tells Dominica that Próspero cannot possibly love her. Later he repents, as he had done when he hurt Delfín: «Antes no hablaba yo; hablaba en mí un espíritu malicioso que, a veces, me posee, me empuja y me dicta palabras que no están en mi corazón» (II, 704). This, of course, is a reference to the dualism of the last two lines of the poem: the power or capacity within the same person to do both harm and good. This dualism in the personality of Arias has been analyzed by Pelayo H. Fernández:

> Va saliendo a la luz, cada vez con mayor claridad, el dualismo anímico de Arias, ángel y diablo a un tiempo. Como ángel «habla con entero juicio»; como diablo, habla en él «un demonio que me adueña y me vuelve insensato». Los dos ángeles que todos los humanos llevamos dentro (las dos caras de la moneda) exigen un equilibrio; pero cuando el ángel malo goza de excesiva libertad —como ocurre en el caso de Arias...—, la conducta del individuo se torna imprevisible y se tiñe de peligrosidad. [24]

The poem introducing chapter eight discusses the dualism of Love which is as old as life and as young: «¡Amor, como la vida viejo! / ¡Moza como la vida, Amor!» (II, 705). The court of Elsingor is attending a feast: the king, the queen, Ophelia and Hamlet. Suddenly Hamlet grabs one of the torches and whirls it around furiously. The last strophe reads:

> ¡Amor! Alumbras, manso o furibundo,
> antorcha roja o recogido foco,
> la tragicomedia del mundo...
> Pero estás en las manos de un loco.
>
> (II, 705)

Love gives meaning and light to this world, but it can also hurt and destroy. Love too is ambiguous, dualistic, and made up of contrary forces. [25]

The prose gives details of Próspero's courtship of Dominica. He comes every evening to sit and talk with her in a cool antechamber of the house in the company of the old nurse. Often Enrique and Fernanda, the king

---

[24] FERNÁNDEZ, p. 125. It will be remembered that Teófilo Pajares also recognized that there was both an angel and a devil in his personality.
[25] AMORÓS, *La novela intelectual*, p. 281.

and queen, are there. Merlo has the gift of words and his flattering speeches to Dominica have her completely enthralled. Her feelings are pictured in the dualistic terms of Petrarchan love poetry: «un fuego inextinguible que lastima y deleita», «esta trasustanciación gloriosa y dolorosa». The only one absent from these evening gatherings is Arias. Influenced by the courtship of his sister, Arias himself has awakened to love. Like many young adolescents, he first loves all women in general, but then finds one woman to adore. Even though he has seen her only three times and does not even know her name, he becomes insane with love for her. It is now clear that the last line of the poem, «estás en las manos de un loco», refers to the love of the mad Arias.

Chapter nine starts with a poem that describes night as the dark womb of all crimes: rape, adultery, murder, theft, cowardice, and fear. Night is the origin of all troubles because «... acogidos a tu seno, / animales y hombres se ayuntan / y, encendidos de un furor ciego, / perpetúan la vida en la tierra» (II, 710). In these lines, the night, usually associated with death, is also the origin of life. The morning bells, like the rooster, celebrate the resurrection of a new day and its triumph over night/death: «¡Que cante el gallo matutino / y caiga Lucifer al infierno!» Nevertheless, night/death has its own triumphs: «Ki ki ri ki. / Amanece otro nuevo día. / Pero alguien ya no podrá verlo.»

In the prose portion of this chapter, Merlo informs the Limón family that he is supposed to visit a widow and her daughter later that night. The two women live alone: «—Gracias a la exquisita tutela de los Limones, dos mujeres pueden vivir solas y seguras en Guadalfranco, aunque sean ricas —aseveró don Enrique» (II, 711). However, the next morning, the widow and her daughter are found murdered in their home. The young girl had been raped and she had received twenty-seven knife wounds. Because the watchman had seen Merlo leave around midnight and his fan and cane are found in the house, he is taken into custody. The whole town rises against the Limón faction, and Enrique Limón, sensing the disaster for his family, dies at the end of chapter nine. The final lines of the poem seem to refer, therefore, both to the deaths of the two women and to that of don Enrique.

In a manner reminiscent of the first chapter of Genesis, the poem to chapter ten describes the darkness that existed in the beginning: «En principio era la sombra; / la sombra letárgica y caótica; / un anonadamiento; la nada cóncava» (II, 714). Then was the Word and the Word brought light: «Surgió el Verbo. Surgió la voz maravillosa. / Y con la voz se hizo la luz, aparecieron las cosas, / se desplegó la acción, nació la historia.» Still, this birth of light is painful: «Se hizo la luz, con dolientes congojas. / Todos los alumbramientos dejan las entrañas rotas.» And this light does not seem strong enough to conquer darkness: «Y, no obstante, había noche tenebrosa. / Porque la luz era el verbo dentro de la sombra.»

The interplay of light/truth versus darkness/guilt expressed metaphorically in the poem will be the main theme of chapter ten.

This chapter recounts the confession of Arias to the murder of Lola and her mother. He tells Dominica that after finally learning the name of the girl he loves, and hearing of Merlo's visit to her house, he follows. After Merlo's departure, Bermudo helps him rape the girl. When her mother appears on the scene, Arias kills the mother and then, in the familiar fit of insane fury, stabs Lola repeatedly. The next morning, when he hears of the murders, he has suppressed his crime to such an extent that he does not realize he is the murderer. It is only after his father's death that he becomes conscious of the truth. The faithful Bermudo («ver-mudo») has of course kept quiet but when Arias asks if what he thought was a dream is in fact real, Bermudo has to nod in agreement. So, brutal reality at last invades the dreamlike existence of Arias's world. His tragedy is the disparity between his dreams of glory and the only concrete action that he manages to carry out:

> Dans ces petits villages silencieux de la Castille, comme dans toute solitude un peu morne, on rêve, et le rêve fait les saints et les révolutionnaires, les héros et les criminels. De l'un à l'autre, il y a moins loin qu'on ne croit, tant est fragile la volonté humaine. Ainsi rêvait l'héritier des Limones... M. Ramón Pérez de Ayala... nous raconte la chute de la noble famille des Limones... et la triste fin d'un de ces rêves héroïques. [26]

In his confession to Dominica, Arias bemoans the fact that Lola never said a word. If she had spoken, he might have come to his senses:

> Lola se había incorporado. Estaba como a cosa de tres pasos de mí. Me escupió y se lanzó después sobre mí, como para sacarme los ojos. Todo sin decir palabra. En todo el tiempo no dijo una palabra. Jamás llegué a oír el sonido de su voz. Si hubiera hablado, creo que no la hubiera matado; se hubiera hecho la luz. Pero no habló, no habló. (II, 717)

The relationship to the introductory poem is obvious—her voice could have been the light that saved him from the darkness. Her silence is also reminiscent of the poem about the doll. He loves Lola: «Era tan suave, tan tibia, tan dulce... Aún se me derriten las entrañas al recordarla, y siento que todavía la tengo entre mis brazos» (II, 716). Nevertheless, he destroys her; her silence is her undoing. Perhaps the lesson to be learned here is that communication (love) is the only way to bridge the darkness/light dualism.

The theme of light and shadow is a leitmotif throughout this novella, and nowhere is it more evident than in this chapter. It begins: «Caía la

---

[26] HENRI GUERLIN, *L'Espagne moderne vue par ses écrivains* (Paris: Perrin et Cie., 1924), p. 10.

tarde. La sombra iba embebiendo y saturando la alcoba de Dominica. Como si la sombra se adensase, cuajándose de improviso, apareció Arias» (II, 714). As Arias goes on with his confession, it gets darker and darker in the room, but his words are a light to the darkness in his soul. When he is condemned to death at the end of the chapter, it seems that darkness has won («Y, no obstante, había noche tenebrosa»), but one is left with the feeling that Arias has at last faced reality and confronted his true self: «Y con la voz se hizo la luz, aparecieron las cosas.» Arias, then, like all men, is composed of darkness and light, but it is words that give light and form (identity) to darkness.

The last poem of *La caída de los Limones* uses again the bells of the second poem, bells which announce the dualism of birth (white) and death (black):

> Brilla el sol con un nuevo hechizo.
> Tañe la campana argentina.
> Es la campana del bautizo.
> Llora de gozo la madrina.
>
> De pronto el cielo se ha nublado.
> Repica el fúnebre esquilón.
> Tañe por un ajusticiado
> la campana de la prisión.
>
> . . . .
>
> Tan-tan. Tan-tan.
> Las campanas en los campanarios
> anuncian al caballero blanco.
> ¡Oh luminoso arcano!
>
> Tan-tan. Tan-tan.
> Las campanas en los cementerios
> anuncian al caballero negro.
> ¡Oh sombrío misterio!
>
> (II, 719)

As Pelayo H. Fernández has pointed out with regard to this poem, «Hay contrapuesto un juego de luces y sonidos que simbolizan la alegría de nacer y la tristeza del morir, polos opuestos que sin embargo, tienen en común ser a la par misterios y atributos del vivir».[27]

In this final chapter one returns to the boarding house in Madrid. The narrator awakens to find that breakfast has not been prepared as usual. When he questions the maid, she answers with a fit of laughter that Mariquita is having pains. «—Pues no veo que sea cosa de risa el que tenga dolores la Mariquita» (II, 720) is the narrator's reaction, until he realizes

[27] FERNÁNDEZ, *Estudios sobre Ramón Pérez de Ayala*, p. 134.

that the pains mean that she is about to give birth. We can see in this passage that birth (and life) is composed of the dualistic elements pain and joy, an idea repeated later when the narrator informs us that «Mariquita dio a luz un niño, feliz y trabajosamente, a las seis de la tarde» (II, 721). This mixture of pleasure and pain is related to the third strophe of the preface poem placed symbolically in the middle, between those about birth and death:

> Apuremos el vaso colmado
> con el vino color de miel.
> En el fondo del vaso hay guardado
> sabor de cicuta y de hiel.

Lunch is such a confusion that no one notices the absence of the two enigmatic ladies, nor are they there at the evening meal. It is only upon reading the newspapers before bedtime that the narrator realizes that their brother and his servant were executed at noon that day. We now understand the message of the bells in the poem; they toll for the birth of Mariquita's child and for the death of Arias and Bermudo.

The play of darkness and light is repeated. Noon, the middle of the day representing the apex of life, is precisely the hour at which death occurs. By contrast, when evening is falling, there is a new life, and it is important that the author uses the phrase «dio a luz» rather than, for example, «el niño nació». Six o'clock in the evening is symbolic because, although to Christians it means the end of the day and the approach of fearful night, to Jews, the evening is the beginning of the new day. It seems that Pérez de Ayala very consciously uses Saturday for these two events. Saturday is the last day of the week for the Jews—the end symbolized by the death of Arias—but six o'clock in the evening signals the approach of the new day, the first day of the week, Sunday, the day of resurrection for the Christians. This is simbolized by the birth of Mariquita's child. The juxtaposition of noon, death/evening, birth, and end (of week)/beginning (of week) is an important step toward the polarity one will find in *Belarmino y Apolonio*. What for some is the middle of life (noon) is death for others, while what is the end for some is the beginning for others. It all depends on the point of view. Birth and death, beginning and end are polar ends of the life cycle symbolized by the full circle made by day and night. Life continues, a life composed of «miel» and «hiel»:

> El último poema insiste en que el misterio de la vida reside en sus contrastes: blanco y negro, hiel y miel..., bautizo y muerte... Es el leitmotif de toda esta novela y una de las creencias más arraigadas en el escritor asturiano. En esto consiste «la tragicomedia del mundo». [28]

[28] AMORÓS, *La novela intelectual*, p. 282.

This novel closes the trilogy of *Tres novelas poemáticas de la vida española*. The author uses the dual voices of poetry and prose in an attempt to create a harmonious whole that will integrate synthetic perception with analytical understanding in order to arrive at a more complete, more universal truth. *Prometeo* imitates the epic style in the poetry but parodies it in the prose, while *Luz de domingo* uses the medieval *romance* for the poetry and allegory for the narrative. The poems of *La caída de los Limones* use a variety of styles, perhaps as a reflection of the eclecticism of the twentieth century. Poem number three, in which the poet laments the decay of Spain's glorious past and of the hidalgos, seems to reflect the style of Antonio Machado; the influence of Rubén Darío is clear in poem four, which describes a young prince and his retinue; while poem six about the doll, in imitation of fairy tale language, starts with the line, «Una vez, érase que se era...». In all three novellas, Pérez de Ayala uses Spain's literary tradition to serve as a contrast to the harsh realities of modern-day Spain:

> La unidad de los tres relatos se encuentra en los moldes literarios que les sirven de fondo y que la anécdota contradice en los tres: el tono épico de *Prometeo* se vierte sobre acciones ridículas y lastimosas; el clima heroico del romancero envuelve acciones cobardes y viles en *Luz de domingo*; el ambiente de cuento de hadas y de tradición en que vive el protagonista de la *La caída de los Limones* propicia una conducta de asesino. El heroísmo, la nobleza, el ideal que corresponden a la épica, al romancero, al cuento de hadas, se transforma en cobardía, vileza y crimen en la vida de los españoles: la discordancia entre el pasado y el presente, entre literatura y vida es un hecho que se subraya trágicamente en las tres novelas poemáticas. [29]

In other words, Pérez de Ayala seems to be using literary tradition to point out a dualism dear to the heart of Spanish literature, that of the ideal versus the real.

The use of poetry and prose to unite the real and metaphorical worlds and thus more nearly approach an ideal artistic reality is an important step in Pérez de Ayala's novelistic career. Pérez de Ayala now seeks what he called «las normas eternas» and the works that follow, and which end his career as a novelist, have been called by Julio Matas his «novelas normativas». [30] They depart from the classical nineteenth-century concept of the novel in that they are not concerned with concrete reality—the reality of the material world is only a backdrop for the «more real» conflicts of the psychological world, and the characters tend to be psychological symbols. Nevertheless, even though his characters are symbols, they are portrayed as very human in the novel that follows, *Belarmino y Apolonio*.

---

[29] MARÍA DEL CARMEN BOBES NAVES, «Ramón Pérez de Ayala, la obra», in *Homenaje a Ramón Pérez de Ayala (1880-1980), Nueva Conciencia* (Mieres del Camino), Nos. 20-21 (October 1980), p. 32.

[30] This is the subtitle of Matas's book *Contra el honor*.

4

BELARMINO Y APOLONIO

Since *Belarmino y Apolonio* is regarded as Pérez de Ayala's best novel, many studies have already been made of it, and repetition of some of what has been said before is inevitable. Particular mention must be made of the work done by Andrés Amorós, Mariano Baquero Goyanes, María del Carmen Bobes, Sara Suárez Solís, and Frances Wyers Weber, each of whom has used the novel for extensive analysis of the author. These critics have concentrated on perspectivism as the main theme of the novel. While perspectivism cannot be denied, we hope to focus on it only from the dualistic point of view (there are many others, as Frances Wyers Weber has proved); the perspectivism in this novel is but a part of the author's continuing preocupation with dualism.

For purposes of clarity, the chapter is divided into various segments under these headings: Opposite Perspectives, Belarmino and Apolonio, The Dualism of Language, Dualistic Perspectives of the Church, Dualisms within One Person, and Miscellaneous Opposites. These subheadings, all interrelated in a continuously shifting pattern, really cannot be separated one from the other. To do so would be an injustice for, in the words of Frances Weber:

> Pérez de Ayala has here devised a complicated mechanism of interchanging parts: two theorists argue about two opposing ways of understanding human reality; three narrators report the action which is divided into two separate but related plots; events take place on two different time levels and are described from distinct points of view, sometimes as fact, sometimes as fiction. The structural complexity perfectly embodies the theme of plural realities. The theory of the double view, introduced in the Prologue and developed in regards to fiction in Chapter II, turns out to be the compositional principle of the entire work. [1]

---

[1] WEBER, *The Literary Perspectivism of Ramón Pérez de Ayala*, p. 64.

OPPOSITE PERSPECTIVES

The first important distinction in the novel is made in the Prologue by don Amaranto de Fraile who separates «la edad científica» from «la edad teológica»:

> Antes, en la edad teológica, el hombre se había acostumbrado a la presencia de lo absoluto en cada realidad relativa... En un árbol, si era laurel, un antiguo veía a Dafne, sentía el contacto invisible de Apolo, y empleaba las hojas para guisar y para coronar los púgiles y los poetas. ¿Qué más necesitaba saber? En la edad científica un solo árbol se multiplicaba en tantos árboles como ciencias, y ninguno es el árbol verdadero. (IV, 17)

He then goes on to explain that each scientist or specialist sees something distinctive in the same tree. It is seen in a different light by the botanist, the architect, the naval engineer, the telegrapher, the economist, the doctor, the chemist, the biologist and so forth. But to don Amaranto the truth is that

> El universo es coordinación de infinitos fenómenos heterogéneos. Cada ciencia, en cambio, se conforma con añascar enteco troje de fenomenillos homogéneos, y obstínase en no admitir que de fuera, aparte, por debajo y por encima de ellos, exista realidad alguna. (IV, 16)

This is but another example of the dichotomy between life (the tree) and reason (the sciences) brought about by reason's need to categorize; categories necessarily divide and separate, and, in so doing, they lose sight of the wholeness of truth:

> The precise order of reality is not for Pérez de Ayala a mere subjective hypothesis which would make it perspectivistic; it is an objective fact, albeit a fact inaccessible to the intellect. Rationality does not lead to total knowledge for it deals with only a small portion of experience. The limitations of reason are evident in the contrast between the analytical functions of science and the synthetic comprehension made possible by theology in earlier, more ingenuous times. [2]

To prove his point, don Amaranto uses the example of a lovely young girl who is eating at the table with them. He believes that he can analyze the girl by describing her biochemical functions, by making a philological study of her speech, or by evaluating her personality according to her horoscope. But in the end, what has he accomplished? Nothing. Nothing, because he has not yet captured the vital essence of her spirit. To do that, he must enter into the private drama of her life:

---

[2] WEBER, p. 17.

¿Qué he conseguido saber sobre esta muchacha? Nada. Nada. Nada. En cambio, si es vecina de mi aposento y a través del frágil tabique la oigo suspirar, reír, llorar, sé que está triste, que goza, que sufre. Otro día cojo al vuelo una frase; otro, percibo un diálogo; otro, hablo con ella y la guío con sutileza a que me confíe algún secretillo; otro, completo lo que ella me haya dicho con lo que otros me comuniquen acerca de ella misma; y así, poco a poco, he llegado a conocerla en puridad, porque he entrado en su drama. (IV, 18-19)

Science, then, is not the way to the whole truth. According to don Amaranto, drama and philosophy—the second important dualism in the novel—are the only two ways to arrive at truth. With drama, it is possible to penetrate the private essence of each individual, and with philosophy, one can amalgamate these various essences into the one true essence. This can even be accomplished by the same person, as don Amaranto himself has experienced:

A veces, extendiendo la mirada sobre mis vecinos de mesa, cuyos dramas privativos se me presentan al pronto con escénica plasticidad, y elevándome en seguida, y como a pesar mío, a contemplarlos filosóficamente, *sub specie aeterni,* me acomete un escalofrío patético, me dan ganas de llorar... (IV, 19)

(This would be an explanation for the «desdoblamiento del personaje» of Alberto and Rosina in the novels of the tetralogy.) But, warns don Amaranto, whether one is dramatically submerged in the forest or philosophically contemplating it from above, because of one's limitations «los árboles estorban ver el bosque» (IV, 19). So, in reality, even drama and philosophy are inadequate, and this inadequacy is at the heart of the many ambiguities presented by *Belarmino y Apolonio.*

Pérez de Ayala has employed several techniques in order to show man's incapacity to perceive the whole of reality. The most important is that of using opposite pairs, a technique he uses throughout his novels. The Prologue is devoted to the ideas of don Amaranto de Fraile, whereas the Epilogue presents the notes left by his opposite, Froilán Escobar. Both have similar names, both are lifelong students in their own way, and both lead ascetic lives. Escobar also thinks that the avenues to knowledge are drama and philosophy, but he and don Amaranto have opposing views regarding their functions. For don Amaranto, drama is vitalist and subjective, whereas philosophy is rational and objective. «These two approaches are, nevertheless, inseparable, for philosophical contemplation inevitably follows dramatic empathy.»[3] For Escobar, on the other hand, the vitalist is the philosopher for he truly experiences pathos, while the dramatist, essentially cold and rational, studies human experience only in order to imitate it.[4]

[3] WEBER, «Relativity and the Novel: Pérez de Ayala's *Belarmino y Apolonio*», *Philological Quarterly,* 43 (1964), 255.

[4] See LEON LIVINGSTONE, «The Theme of the *Paradoxe sur le Comédien* in the Novels of Pérez de Ayala», *Hispanic Review,* 22 (1954), 208-23. Escobar quotes Diderot in his defense. This idea was presented earlier by Pérez de Ayala in *Troteras*

But in the end, drama and philosophy are also ambiguous and therefore as inadequate as either theology or science:

> El narrador no se preocupa por definir qué entiende por drama ni qué entiende por filosofía; se limita, en el prólogo, a exponer las opiniones de don Amaranto, que las defiende como formas de conocimiento y, en el epílogo, a reproducir las notas de Froilán Escobar, que trata de analizar los caracteres del filósofo y el dramaturgo. Las opiniones de don Amaranto y el estudiantón son contrapuestas y, en medio, dice el narrador, «se extienden sinnúmero infinito de otras verdades inmediatas». Drama y filosofía son, por tanto, conceptos ambiguos... [5]

Perhaps that is why don Amaranto always feels like weeping when he views human drama *sub specie aeterni,* even though he maintains that the essence of philosophy is equanimity. What is happening here is that the clear-cut dualisms of the early tetralogy are now becoming blurred into interchangeable polarities as exemplified by what Belarmino says to Monsieur Colignon:

> —Usted es la materia; yo soy el espíritu. Usted se alegra con las cosas; yo, alejándome de las cosas. Usted es el sí y yo el no. O, si usted quiere, usted es el no y yo el sí. ¿Soy yo superior a usted? Nada de eso. Ni el sí es superior al no, ni el no es superior al sí... (IV, 102-03)

For this reason, it is perfectly acceptable to find contradictions in don Amaranto's statements because he is a philosopher and therefore understands the contradictions inherent in human nature:

> The novel re-examines the question of which perspective—that of the philosopher Belarmino or that of the dramatist Apolonio—is really the spectator's and which the actor's. Even this question is treated in dualistic terms, for the prologue and the epilogue... adopt contradictory attitudes to the very attitudes represented by the incompatible cobblers. [6]

The narrator uses the points of view of don Amaranto and Escobar «porque entre ellos cabe inscribir todos los demás, ya que, por ser los más antitéticos, son los más comprensivos» (IV, 218). He then continues «La doctrina de don Amaranto es refutable y no menos defendible, y otro tanto la de Escobar. Y en resolución, todas las opiniones humanas. El error es de aquellos que piden que una opinión humana posea verdad absoluta» (IV, 218). [7] The point of the novel is precisely that contradictions can and should be reconciled:

---

y *danzaderas* in which an actor friend carefully observes the death of Teófilo Pajares in order to go home and imitate his facial expressions in front of a mirror.

[5] RAFAEL NÚÑEZ RAMOS, «La unidad de Belarmino y Apolonio», in *Homenaje a Ramón Pérez de Ayala* (Oviedo: Universidad de Oviedo, Servicio de Publicaciones, 1980), pp. 126-27.

[6] BROWN, pp. 40-41.

[7] This is similar to Ortega's idea that Truth is a summary of the various perspectives of all views possible.

> Consecuentemente, los conceptos de drama y filosofía no pueden iluminar
> unívocamente el carácter de los personajes, porque los conceptos son relativos
> y ambiguos. Según la perspectiva que adoptemos, la de don Amaranto o la de
> Escobar, podremos profundizar, en uno u otro sentido, en el carácter de Belar-
> mino y Apolonio. Si todas las perspectivas fueran posibles simultáneamente,
> Belarmino y Apolonio se confundirían: serían ambos dramaturgo y filósofo
> juntamente. [8]

In the second chapter, the narrator explains that he had heard the
story of Belarmino and Apolonio and wished to write about it, but found
himself frustrated by the limitations of the written word which, because
it is lineal in space and time, can only describe superficially, whereas the
narrator would have liked to describe a scene or a character from all
points of view at the same time. (This is exactly what the cubists were
trying to do in art.) He appeals for help to the *sombra* of don Amaranto, who provides some guidelines. Earlier, don Amaranto had described
science as seeing reality with the fly's compound viewing structure which
fragments reality into a mosaic vision. Now don Amaranto talks about the
monovision of the cyclops which may be related to the theological view:

> Los cíclopes, por ver el mundo superficialmente, quisieron asaltar el Olimpo;
> pero los dioses los precipitaron en el hondo Tártaro... Ahora bien: describir es
> como ver con un ojo, paseándolo por la superficie de un plano, porque las imá-
> genes son sucesivas en el tiempo, y no se funden, ni superponen, ni, por lo
> tanto, adquieren profundidad. (IV, 33)

However, man, having passed through the inadequacies of both the theological and scientific views, is no longer satisfied with either because, says
don Amaranto,

> El hombre, con ser más mezquino, aventaja al cíclope, a causa de poseer dos
> ojos con que ve en profundidad el mundo sensible... La visión propia del hom-
> bre, que es la visión diafenomenal, como quiera que, porque enfocar el objeto
> con cada ojo desde un lado, lo penetra en ángulo y recibe dos imágenes late-
> rales que se confunden en una imagen central, es una visión en profundidad.
> (IV, 33-34)

From now on in the novels of Pérez de Ayala, this is going to be the key:
man himself is the integrator of reality. Instead of the mosaic vision of the
fly and the monovision of the cyclops, man has a dual vision that allows
him depth perception and perspective. Yet man, as one will see more
clearly in *Tigre Juan,* also has physical limitations which make complete
integration almost impossible. The one who comes closest to it, in the
opinion of Pérez de Ayala, is the painter. The author, himself a painter,
knows of what he speaks when he has don Amaranto say:

[8] NÚÑEZ RAMOS, pp. 137-38.

El novelista, en cuanto hombre, ve las cosas estereoscópicamente, en profundidad; pero en cuanto artista, está desprovisto de medios con que reproducir su visión. No puede pintar; únicamente puede describir, enumerar. La misión de ver con mayor profundidad, delicadeza y emoción y enseñar a los otros a ver de la propia suerte, le toca al pintor... El pintor, a la inversa del novelista, no se deja dominar por la vastedad del objeto, sino que lo domina. (IV, 34)

In the end, the narrator gets impatient with don Amaranto's ramblings and asks him how to describe the Rúa Ruera of Pilares where the two cobblers live. Don Amaranto answers: «—No describiéndola. Busca la visión diafenomenal. Inhíbete en tu persona de novelista. Haz que otras dos personas la vean al propio tiempo, desde ángulos laterales contrapuestos» (IV, 34-35). The two persons whom the narrator chooses to describe the Rúa Ruera are Juan Lirio, a painter, and Pedro Lario, a sociologist.

The contrasts between these two men are immediately observable even in their names. The gentle and delicate disciple of Christ as opposed to the choleric and burly St Peter are evoked by the names Juan y Pedro, and the last names have several possible meanings: Lirio is the lily, symbolizing the ethereal or spiritual side of man, and there is also the suggestion of *lírico*, the poetic expression of man's emotions. On the other hand, Lario evokes the hearth and home, the comforts that satisfy man's material and prosaic nature. There is also a play on vowels: the closed *i* suggests thinness whereas the *a*, the most open of the vowels, suggests rotundity. [9] These names might also suggest «the Theosophist's theory in which man is composed of a dense body and an ethereal body or double, magnetically bonded». [10]

Pedro Lario is representative of the scientific view. He happens to be a Spencerian sociologist, but he could have been an architect or a civil engineer. The point is that he sees the Rúa Ruera from a single, rationalist point of view, with preconceived notions about what constitutes absolute perfection:

Ahora bien: la idea, el concepto de la ciudad aparece cuando el hombre comprende que por encima del capricho impulsivo de su arbitrio personal están la utilidad y el decoro colectivos, el propósito común de prosperidad, cultura y deleite, en los cuales participan por obligación y derecho cuantos en la ciudad conviven. Antes de llegar a este punto, el hombre arraiga en aldehuelas salvajes o posa en aduares nómadas. Mas ya que el individuo se aplica a realizar el concepto de una ciudad, es decir, de un esquema, una estructura, con propósitos ideales,... surge la ciudad helénica, arquetipo de urbes; surgen la norma, el canon, la simetría... (IV, 37)

[9] Telephone conversation with Dr Thomas Montgomery, Department of Spanish and Portuguese, Tulane University, 12 January 1984.
[10] WILMA NEWBERRY, «Ramón Pérez de Ayala's Concept of the *Doppelgänger* in *Belarmino y Apolonio*», *Symposium*, 34 (1980), 60.

Pedro Lario finds the Rúa Ruera ugly because it does not follow the logical, orderly laws of the universe. Man, according to him, destroys the inherent order of the universe: «El advenimiento del hombre... en medio de la Naturaleza, trae aparejados el desorden, la discordia, las dudas y confusiones...» (IV, 38). The reason man does this, says Lario, is because man puts himself at the center of the universe instead of seeing all things in their relativistic proportions. And man does so because of his fear of death, which Lario finds absurd:

> La lógica humana, en su origen, es rudimentaria e ilógica, porque procede por tanteos y no en derechura ni con seguridad. Débese ello a que durante esta etapa el hombre anda buscando finalidades absolutas, en lugar de coordinaciones experimentales y finalidades relativas; y todo porque tiene miedo a la muerte, pusilanimidad desconocida en la Naturaleza hasta el nacimiento de la conciencia humana. (IV, 39)

For Pedro, the answer lies in accepting the finality of existence and submitting to the «lógica cósmica», thus becoming one with Nature.

Juan Lirio vehemently disagrees. He represents life as opposed to Pedro's positivistic reason, and he finds the Rúa Ruera beautiful precisely because it reflects all the incongruities of life itself:

> —En cuanto a la belleza de los griegos, te respondo que a la nariz, en mármol de Paros, de una estatua, prefiero la nariz respingadilla y de aletas palpitantes de esa chatunga que sube por la calle. Y en cuanto a la belleza lógica del mundo, te respondo que me atraen más las obras del hombre que las de la Naturaleza. Me gusta más una góndola que un tiburón...
> —Has caído en contradicción. Prefieres la chata a la estatua; y la chata es una obra de la Naturaleza. Prefieres la góndola al tiburón porque la góndola es obra del hombre.
> —Sobre las obras de la Naturaleza pongo las del hombre, y sobre las del hombre, la vida misma, y con preferencia la fuente de la vida: la mujer. Pero concedo que me contradigo con frecuencia. ¿Y qué? Así me siento vivir. Si no me contradijese y obedeciese a pura lógica, sería un fenómeno de naturaleza y no me sentiría vivir. (IV, 35-36)

Thus, Juan Lirio, like Unamuno, defends the contradiction and the paradox:

> Amo la vida porque temo la muerte. Amo el Arte porque es la expresión más íntima y completa de la vida. Pongo el Arte sobre la Naturaleza, porque la Naturaleza, no sabiendo que de continuo se está muriendo, es una realidad inexpresiva y muerta. El árbol amarillo de otoño ignora que se muere; yo soy quien lo sabe, cuando en un cuadro perpetúo su agonía. El Arte vivifica las cosas,... las satura de esa contradicción radical que es la vida, puesto que la vida es al propio tiempo negación y afirmación de la muerte. (IV, 40)

As they talk, Juan busily sketches the street scene and when he has finished, Pedro is astonished at the beauty of the drawing: «—La calle no puede ser más fea. El dibujo no puede ser más hermoso» (IV, 41). There are several paradoxes in this statement. First, the Rúa Ruera, an everchanging, incongruous reality, is like life itself. However, Juan's portrayal, using technical ability based on reason, makes these incongruities harmonious. Although Juan defends life, in the very act of trying to perpetuate it, he has had to make it reasonable. On the other hand, Pedro, who defended a harmonious archetype of a street, through Juan's sketch has to concede the beauty of its incongruities. There are thus the two interchangeable poles of life and reason, and the concession that one cannot do without the other. It seems important, nevertheless, to point out that in either case the force that integrates both life and reason is man himself.

In a similar fashion, there are three narrative lines: Angustias's, Pedro's, and the narrator's; and it is the reader who integrates all three. Angustias's version is short and dry: «A mí me perdió un cura» (IV, 26); Pedro attempts to justify what happened; and the narrator describes the background of the incident. The three narratives are not contradictory as to facts, but they do represent the dual poles of subjectivity/objectivity and drama/philosophy. Angustias's version is devoid of emotion except when she defends Pedro against the narrator's invective. Pedro's version, especially toward the end, is deeply emotional:

> Y tú, hermana mía..., ¿dónde estás, en qué oscura mazmorra te encerré, a ciegas, que no doy con la entrada, aunque sangran mis pies de tanto caminar y mis manos de tanto tropezar a tientas? Te busqué y no te he encontrado; te esperé y no has venido. Mi alma estará triste hasta la muerte; muertos mis oídos a las campanas de resurrección; muertos mis ojos a los colores de primavera. (IV, 192)

The versions of Angustias and Pedro would be subjective because they have actually experienced the drama. The narrator's, on the other hand, would be from the philosophical or objective viewpoint since he can give a complete picture of the events. However, it should be pointed out that the versions of Angustias and Pedro, although not opposites, are nevertheless different: that of Angustias might be considered behaviorist and Pedro's dramatic. Don Amaranto's description of the girl in the boarding house, and Angustias's version, give only external details; we need Pedro's view to get an inner vision of the drama, and we need the philosophical panorama to gain the complete picture. [11]

The three narrators tell two plots—Belarmino's rivalry with Apolonio and the elopement of Pedro and Angustias. Again, there is a fluctuation between a subjective and an objective account. Thus, in the story of the

---

[11] FERNÁNDEZ, «El prólogo en Belarmino y Apolonio», Boletín del Instituto de Estudios Asturianos (Oviedo), núm. 78 (1973), 145-46.

elopement, the narrator presents the objective view of the incident, as seen from the eyes of the two shoemakers and the other people in the town. It is objective in that the reader does not enter into the feelings of the two young lovers. However, in the next chapter, not only have the two lovers received their real names (Pedrito and Angustias instead of don Guillén and «la Pinta»), but one is allowed a view of their private drama:

> By giving two versions of an incident the author can show it both from within and from without, subjectively and objectively... The turning point in the lives of both pairs of characters, Belarmino-Apolonio, Pedro-Angustias, is the elopement of the latter... Since in the drama of Belarmino and Apolonio the sentiments of Angustias and Pedro are relatively unimportant, the author focuses only on the thoughts and acts of the shoemakers. But in chapter VII... don Guillén recounts the episode as protagonist: now the mad cobblers recede into the background while the feelings of the actor-narrator occupy the foreground. The subjective and objective elements in the two stories are reversible... [12]

The two time lines, past and present, can also be related to subjectivity and objectivity. The objective narrator relates events in the past; the subjective narrator (don Guillén) tells the story in the present. But the true or complete story is actually a fusion of the objective past and subjective present, and this fusion is accomplished by the reader who thus re-creates the story, to use Unamuno's expression. Again, it is man's mind (the reader's) which integrates the disparate realities:

> La sensación que busca crear es la de simultaneidad y absoluta actualidad, puesto que al barajar los diversos tiempos se transmite a cada uno de ellos algo que pertenece a los demás. Es precisamente en ese tiempo totalizador de la narración (y por lo tanto atemporal) donde se salva y eterniza la historia de Belarmino y Apolonio. [13]

In other words, the reader can see the drama *sub specie aeterni*. Don Amaranto's theories become, therefore, a key to the structure of the book. On the other hand, Escobar's ideas provide the basis for an understanding of its principal characters, the philosopher Belarmino and the dramatist Apolonio.

BELARMINO AND APOLONIO

Don Amaranto had said that the philosopher witnesses reality objectively whereas the dramatist experiences it subjectively. Froilán Escobar, in the Epilogue, has a view that is quite the contrary:

[12] WEBER, «Relativity and the Novel», p. 261.
[13] FERNÁNDEZ, «El prólogo en Belarmino y Apolonio», pp. 143-44.

La cualidad primordial del dramaturgo (léase Apolonio) es la aptitud para la simulación eficaz. Esta simulación no es sólo externa y de superficie. El dramaturgo, desde el fondo de su propia alma, comienza a simular para consigo mismo; pero el *ego* más recóndito y personal permanece siempre ausente e inhibido de la emoción... Hay una paradoja del dramaturgo; es la misma que Diderot llamó paradoja del comediante. La emoción no se comunica, sino que se provoca. Para provocar una emoción hay que mantenerse frío. Hacen llorar los actores que saben fingir el llanto. Los que lloran de veras hacen reír. Lo mismo con el dramaturgo... Diríase que este don de invención (inventar significa descubrir) proviene de que el dramaturgo vive los dramas. Al contrario. El que vive un drama no ve *el* drama; ve *su* drama individual. Y si por caso al dramaturgo le acontece ser víctima en un drama vivo, él permanece ecuánime, sereno. Finge ser actor siempre; y siempre es espectador, espectador de sí mismo. Tal es la paradoja del dramaturgo...

Providencialmente, frente al dramaturgo está el filósofo (léase Belarmino). El filósofo se halla constituido a la inversa del dramaturgo. Por de fuera, serenidad, impasibilidad; en lo más secreto, ardor inextinguible. El filósofo es un energúmeno conservado entre hielo... El filósofo vive todos los dramas; jamás es espectador. El dolor ajeno lo siente como dolor propio; el dolor propio lo multiplica por todos los dolores ajenos; y así en el dolor propio como en el ajeno experimenta el contacto de esta y aquella brasa de la gran hoguera que es el dolor universal, el drama de la vida. (IV, 216-17)

There is ample evidence in the novel that Pérez de Ayala was using the two cobblers to embody Escobar's theories on drama and philosophy. As an example of the fact that the dramatist «desde el fondo de su propia alma, comienza a simular para consigo mismo», we have the scene in which Apolonio goes to tell the Duchess of the elopement: «En el fondo, tan en el fondo que ni él mismo se daba cuenta, Apolonio se sentía orgullosísimo, creyéndose en aquellos momentos un personaje trágico de verdad e imaginando inspirar a la duquesa fuerte interés patético» (IV, 136). And, as an example of the fact that the dramatist remains serene when a real drama happens to him, we have the description of Apolonio's reaction to his son's letter:

Y ahora sí que Apolonio quedó como una estatua, no ya en los ojos, sino en todos sus miembros, y con el alma pálida y vacía. Cuando al fin le volvió la sangre a circular, dijo a la fámula:
—No se cena hoy...
Se dirigió a casa de la duquesa de Somavia... (IV, 135-36)

This is quite different from Belarmino's reaction to the news: «Belarmino se llevó las manos al corazón, dobló la cabeza y sollozó» (IV, 144). Apolonio recovered almost immediately: «Hasta pensaba en los nietecitos» (IV, 137). In the end he opposes the marriage only because Angustias is the daughter of his hated rival. Belarmino, on the other hand, is ready at any time to forgive Angustias, even if she has disgraced the family. And Belarmino never recovers from the loss of his daughter: «Entonces fue cuando Belarmino abandonó la profesión filosófica y ya no remendó más zapatos» (IV, 163).

Belarmino and Apolonio have many opposite characteristics:

1. Belarmino is thin, Apolonio is fat.

2. Belarmino dresses conservatively; Apolonio is flashy.

3. Belarmino has psychological clairvoyance and understands immediately that the Dominican fathers are trying to bribe him; Apolonio is «inocente y sencillo» and therefore does not perceive that the duchess is making fun of him.

4. Belarmino's greatest joy as a cobbler is to restore old shoes—the older, the better; Apolonio prides himself on his handiwork as a shoemaker, for he considers shoes an artistic form.

5. Belarmino never goes to church: Apolonio goes every Sunday without fail.

6. Belarmino loves his «daughter» as if he himself had borne her —«hija de mis entrañas». He feels as if he were both father and mother to her, even though he is only her uncle. Apolonio, on the other hand, is essentially indifferent to his son. While Pedrito is growing up in the Pazo, Apolonio lives in Santiago de Compostela. As a result of his separation, Pedro says that his father is a stranger to him. Apolonio forbids the friendship between Angustias and his son, but Pedro says that «como no se enteraba de nada, no le hice caso». (We are not told whether Belarmino is aware of his daughter's friendship with Pedro, but the inference is that he knows and is not opposed to it.)

7. Belarmino speaks a hermetic language composed of what might be called poetic conceits; Apolonio's language consists of poetic platitudes.

8. Belarmino uses few words because, for him, each word has a multiplicity of meanings. From Apolonio comes a constant flow of words that are often devoid of meaning.

As Andrés Amorós has pointed out, however, Belarmino and Apolonio are not just unilateral opposites. They may be symbols, but they are also characters of flesh and blood:

> Ayala parece preferir un tipo de realismo en el que los individuos, además de su valor singular claramente acusado, posean un carácter significativo que exceda su individualidad... Entre esos dos polos—valor individual, valor simbólico—se van a mover muchas de sus creaciones narrativas. Subrayemos que Ayala concede la primacía al valor individual (la vida auténtica de un personaje) que sólo por añadidura asumirá un contenido general, simbólico. Nada más lejos, por lo tanto, del alegorismo frío que exige una seca traducción matemática: tal personaje *es* tal sentimiento o problema. [14]

[14] AMORÓS, *La novela intelectual*, pp. 69-70.

Precisely because Belarmino and Apolonio are so human, they embody the contradictions inherent in all men. Although dissimilar, they also have many things in common:

1. Contrary to the opinion of Escobar, Apolonio, according to Pedro, is very sensitive: «Mi padre ha tenido siempre una sensibilidad excesiva. Cualquiera cosa le agitaba. Se enternecía por fútiles motivos hasta las lágrimas» (IV, 74). On the other hand, Belarmino is surprisingly studied when he decides to put order into his inner world by negating the existence, in the outer world, of persons who make him unhappy: Xuantipa, Bellido, Apolonio, and Pedro, the seducer of Angustias.

2. Apolonio was forced to abandon his schooling because his teachers found in him an excess of imagination that prevented disciplined work. In similar fashion, Belarmino eventually abandons shoemaking, delighting, instead, in letting his imagination create new meanings for words.

3. Belarmino uses metaphors to create his new meanings so that he is at least as much a poet as Apolonio.

4. This metaphorical creation brings philosophical serenity to Belarmino just as poetry brings equanimity to Apolonio: «Mi padre... respiraba en verso. Esta peculiaridad, o si usted quiere manía, acaso haya sido causa de sus infortunios, pero ciertamente merced a ella los ha sobrellevado con pasmosa resignación e indiferencia» (IV, 75).

5. Apolonio has acquired his erudition orally, from conversations with students in Santiago; Belarmino has acquired his learning from the dictionary, but the erudition of both is «disparatada y pintoresca» (IV, 78).

6. It is almost impossible for Apolonio to speak in prose instead of poetry; likewise, Belarmino has to make a supreme effort to speak in ordinary Spanish instead of in his metaphorical language.

7. Both men keep birds—Belarmino has a magpie, and Apolonio roosters.

8. Both are impractical in business matters.

9. They both react negatively to the shop selling factory-made shoes opened by Martínez. For Belarmino, each shoe is an individual creation, made to fit a particular person; for Apolonio, shoes are a work of art. Therefore, shoes made for a faceless buyer and shoes not made by hand are displeasing to the two protagonists.

In short, these two men are not as opposite as they would appear at first glance:

> The insensibility of the actor-dramatist and the emotionalism of the philosopher are not separable, mutually exclusive attitudes, but reciprocal forces within the same individual... It is only in a purely intellectualized scheme that complete antitheses exist independently. Diderot's theory of the paradox is presented abstractly, out of context; Ayala places it in the context of life, for life,

and its expression in art, is a contradictory, vital fusion of hostile forces welded into an organic unit. [15]

Their unity is also implied in their names. Apolonio could refer to the poet Apollonius of Rhodes and also to the philosopher Apollonius of Tyana. Belarmino is an evident allusion to Cardinal Bellarmine, a famous Jesuit scholar of the late sixteenth century, considered one of the most learned men of his time and, thus, a philosopher. According to don Guillén, the Cardinal also helped edit the second edition of the Breviary under Clement VIII and perhaps wrote some of its hymns. This would make Cardinal Bellarmine a poet as well as a philosopher, just as the name Apolonio suggests both. The separation between the two men comes from the fact that Apollonius of Rhodes preferred lengthy poems in the style of Homer, whereas the Breviary, by its very title, would indicate a synthesizing process. Again, the relationship with the two cobblers is clear: Belarmino synthesizes language metaphorically while Apolonio expresses himself with verbosity. The fact that the two men can be considered both poets and philosophers is mentioned by don Guillén (significantly in the same paragraph in which he speaks of Cardinal Bellarmine): «Él [Belarmino] decía profesar la filosofía, pero yo digo que tenía mucho de poeta; así como mi padre, Apolonio, que decía profesar la dramaturgia, tenía mucho de filósofo» (IV, 172).

It is interesting that Watts quotes Cardinal Bellarmine in his study of dualism in Christianity. Watts points out that this dualism inevitably becomes polaristic in speaking of two Catholic theologians (one of whom is the Cardinal), who,

> in attempting a logical justification of the existence of so excruciating a Hell in the same universe that contains the Beatific Vision of Love Itself, they have let slip the inevitable conclusion that Heaven and Hell are polar and thus mutually sustaining. The *sine qua non* of absolute goodness is absolute evil. [16]

It seems significant that it is with this novel that Pérez de Ayala has shifted from a dualistic vision of the world to one that is polaristic.

The fact that Belarmino and Apolonio are opposites but have so much in common has been studied by Wilma Newberry who calls this phenomenon the «concept of the *Doppelgänger*» or contrastive double. With regard to the two shoemakers, she says:

> Finally, the intricacy of the situation is intensified by one of the paradoxes of contrastive doubles—their differences striking as they may be, fade into the background when their basic sameness is recognized. Since they really constitute parts of a whole..., this is not so paradoxical as it may seem... The main characteristic shared by Belarmino and Apolonio that supersedes all the important

[15] LIVINGSTONE, «The Theme of the *Paradoxe sur le Comédien*», pp. 222-23.
[16] WATTS, p. 181.

differences between them... is their identical attitude to life—they are indifferent
to material values. Instead, they focus... on something beyond the concrete world,
something transcendental... [17]

Newberry also points out that the frequent slaying of the double in
literature is really a form of suicide. Brought to mind is the scene in which
Belarmino catches Apolonio filling his bottle of Vichy water with regular
water from the tap. Apolonio's first instinct is to kill Belarmino: «Por la
frente dramática de Apolonio cruza un negro pensamiento. Ahí está Belarmino, desmedrado e inerme, a su merced. Un botellazo en la cabeza, y
asunto concluido» (IV, 210). But, first, he decides to make Belarmino envious by showing him the telegram from Pedro:

> Pero antes de rematar a Belarmino, saciando así un viejo afán de venganza,
> cuyos motivos, por más que ha rebuscado, Apolonio no ha conseguido encon-
> trarlos en su corazón, ocúrresele humillarlo, rebajarlo cumplidamente, haciendo
> que por primera y última vez le envidie. (IV, 210-11)

Actually the one who has suffered from envy throughout the novel is Apolonio, not Belarmino. (At the end of the novel, Belarmino says that he too
has been envious of Apolonio, but there is no evidence of it in the text.)

Envy is at the root of Apolonio's inexplicable hatred for Belarmino.
Pedro explains that this envy first arose because his father, in Santiago,
had become accustomed to being surrounded and listened to by students;
in Pilares, however, it is Belarmino who is the center of that «ambiente
de ilustración» (IV, 86). Apolonio is jealous of Belarmino's fame, his *público*. His fighting cocks play a significant role in this envy. Their deaths
satisfy in Apolonio the murder-suicide impulse that is common with a double, and his serenity with regard to these losses gives him a sort of fame
which helps to assuage him:

> Como Apolonio perdía siempre, se le iba desnivelando el presupuesto mu-
> cho más de lo prudente. Apolonio no paraba atención en los descalabros eco-
> nómicos mientras su actividad pública, como gallero, le sirviera para ensanchar
> la nombradía; prefería la ruina y la inopia a la oscuridad. Todo lo aceptaba
> con tal de gratificar en alguna medida su vanidad inocente, con tal que se le
> conociese y se hablase de él. Su obsesión era aventajar la fama de Belarmino,
> humillarle algún día. (IV, 121)

This is the Cain and Abel relationship studied by Unamuno in *Abel Sán-
chez*. In the Unamuno novel, Joaquín, a doctor, is supposed to represent
the sciences or reason; Abel, the artist, symbolizes the spirit. But as the
novel develops, at least from Joaquín's point of view (we are never presented Abel's) we come to realize that the passionate, living spirit dwells
in Joaquín and that Abel uses his coldly-studied techniques solely for the

[17] NEWBERRY, p. 65.

purpose of making a good living. It is precisely because Joaquín is so passionate, so vital, that he hates Abel whose fame and glory detract from
his own reputation. For someone as vitalist as Joaquín (and Unamuno)
there can be no half measures. Apolonio has much of Joaquín's passionate
vitality, and we disagree with Escobar that he is a mere observer of life.
Apolonio wants to live, and live completely. Every situation is savored to
the fullest. It is symbolic that he would want to have Vichy water, since
water is the symbol of life. Its most important function is to make the
other inmates envious, a sure sign to him that he has more «life» than they.

But this water symbol, typical of Pérez de Ayala, cannot be unilateral.
At the end of the novel, Apolonio fills his bottle with «agua apócrifa» from
the tap. Actually, as a symbol of life, water from the tap would do as well;
what is really apocryphal is the Vichy label on the bottle. The implication
is that, even though Apolonio might represent life, sometimes that life is
falsified by the dramatist's need for ostentation.

Belarmino, however, remains true to himself. If Apolonio is representative of life, then Belarmino would represent reason or the intellect. As
such, he would have no vitalist need for fame, like Apolonio. Indeed, he
is hardly conscious of his reputation among the students in Pilares. But,
when they are united, each man admits to having been envious of the other.
This illustrates the inherent contradictions within the characters: Apolonio
is not completely life—some of his life is «apócrifa» or a studied pose.
Belarmino is not completely intellect or he would not feel passions like
envy.

Their envy has a deep and unknown source; they do not understand
why they are rivals but they recognize each other instantly when they are
finally united under the laurel trees: «Es la primera vez que se hablan, y se
tratan de tú con espontaneidad, porque en el misterio del pecho eran íntimos el uno del otro desde hace muchos años» (IV, 211). They realize
that they are polar doubles—polar in that they are constantly changing
positions—and that they need each other to be complete:

>—Eres como mi otra mitad.
>—Sí, y tú mi otro testaferro. (Testaferro = hemisferio.) (IV, 212)

Belarmino seems to intuit the close relationship between envy and love
because, for him, *besar* means *envidiar*. (It seems to me that *besar* also has
the implication of robbing someone else of his life, his *aliento*.) The two
halves are united and both are of equal value. Belarmino could have said
to Apolonio the same thing he said to Colignon: «Usted es el sí y yo el
no. O, si usted quiere, usted es el no y yo el sí.» And Monsieur Colignon
says of both: «Belarmino es un grande hombre, y Apolonio, él es también
un otro grande hombre. Yo quiero mostrarles cuánto les amo y les ad-
miro» (IV, 199).

The Dualism of Language

It was noted earlier in this chapter that Belarmino's language is composed of metaphorical conceits of his own creation, whereas Apolonio speaks in well-worn poetic platitudes. «Both are obsessed by words.» [18]

Leon Livingstone, continuing with the thesis of the *Paradoxe sur le Comédien,* points out the inauthenticity of Apolonio's language which is «sólo un instrumento para el 'hacerse interesante'. En cambio, el de Belarmino, elude cuidadosamente lo decorativo en su búsqueda de un medio de comunicación con la verdad, de una avenida a la autenticidad personal». [19] The problem, he says, is the contradictory role of language which, while it is the best instrument for communication with others, nevertheless impedes true communication with one's own authentic self. The reason is that, as soon as we use words to describe ourselves, we become actors, we become doubles—the one who feels the drama and the other who analyzes and tries to interpret it. (This is similar to the case of Juan Lirio who, in using technical ability to depict life, actually deforms it.) Silence, then, is the only way to reach one's true self, and it explains Belarmino's silence as opposed to Apolonio's verbosity. Yet silence and verbosity, philosopher and dramatist, are both necessary for completeness:

> Sinceridad y pose son igualmente necesarios como elementos integrantes de la creación artística. En el arte, en fin, no se trata de fingir o sentir sino de sentir y fingir; o más exactamente de sentir fingiendo. ... Y lo mismo ocurre en el caso del lenguaje. El lenguaje expresivo, sin el control de la sinceridad resulta verbosidad huera, palabrería superficial, ampulosidad vana. Pero, por otra parte, el silencio sólo es la negación de toda posibilidad de comunicación y en este sentido la aniquilación del lenguaje. [20]

Thus, the first dualism of language is its use by the actor versus the philosopher.

The second dualistic element of language is the opposing linguistic theories of the Positivists and the Idealists studied by M. K. Read. The Neogrammarians of the nineteenth century (Positivists) had «a view of linguistic change as governed by blind phonetic laws, explicable in terms of collective as distinct from individual influence, and functioning on the level of the subconscious...». For the Neolinguists (Idealists), on the other hand, language

---

[18] Murray Baumgarten and Gabriel Berns, Introduction to *Belarmino y Apolonio,* by Ramón Pérez de Ayala (Berkeley: University of California Press, 1971), pp. vii.

[19] Leon Livingstone, «Lenguaje y silencio en *Belarmino y Apolonio*», in *Simposio Internacional Ramón Pérez de Ayala, 1880-1980,* ed. Pelayo H. Fernández (Gijón: Imprenta Flores, 1981), p. 81.

[20] Livingstone, p. 89.

is not an entity in its own right, which can be studied «objectively», but a perpetually changing, living reality. Unlike the Neogrammarians, the Neolinguists concentrated on semantic phenomena, and characteristically saw linguistic change as deriving from largely conscious and willful spiritual acts, as aesthetic choices of the individual. [21]

Belarmino would be representative of the Neolinguists and, as we shall see later, Father Alesón would incorporate the ideas of the Neogrammarians. What is necessary is a union between the concern for form of the grammarians and the interest in semantics of the linguists. «And when Belarmino and Apolonio finally come together in embrace, their union seems from a linguistic standpoint to indicate symbolically the necessity of both meaning and form as ingredients of language.» [22] Read also mentions that Spanish linguists have traditionally «refused to surrender unconditionally to Positivism or Idealism» and that, for this reason, they have «provided a context favourable to the working out of a synthesis». [23]

Another aspect of language which is related to the Neogrammarians and the Neolinguists is the conventional status of language defended by Aristotle as opposed to the Platonic view, which emphasizes «the natural relationship between word and thing...». [24] The Platonic view, says Read, would explain the use of nicknames in *Belarmino y Apolonio*: «Los apodos son, cuándo biografía sucinta, cuándo retrato en miniatura. Los dos apodos de Froilán Escobar [el Estudiantón y el Aligator] le historiaban y le retrataban» (IV, 103).

Belarmino is a Platonist—his whole theory of language is that, when we invent a word, we create the thing that it represents. Thus, the thing exists as such because we have a word for it, and not the other way around. The dictionary, for him, is the cosmos because it contains all things. But when he studies the dictionary, Belarmino is very careful not to look at the meaning of the word; instead, he creates his own meanings metaphorically. The problem is that these metaphors are so personal that his language is incomprehensible to others, and he consequently loses the most important function of language which is communication:

> Modernas investigaciones sobre el origen de las metáforas demuestran que la tendencia primitiva a hacer, a través de ellas, más claro y expresivo el pensamiento de los hombres, acaba por hacer más difícil y oscura su lengua. Lo metafórico, que es evidencia y claridad meridiana para él, constituye en el lenguaje de Belarmino la base esencial de su oscuridad. [25]

[21] M. K. READ, «*Belarmino y Apolonio* and the modern linguistic tradition», *Bulletin of Hispanic Studies*, 55 (1978), 330.
[22] READ, p. 334.
[23] READ, p. 331.
[24] READ, p. 330.
[25] CARLOS CLAVERÍA, «Apostillas al lenguaje de Belarmino», in *Cinco estudios de literatura española moderna* (Salamanca: Colegio Trilingüe de la Universidad, 1945), p. 83.

Belarmino's goal is to find one word that would incorporate all things. In this attempt, he is both poet and mystic:

> The poetic, mythical, or mystical mode of vision perceives orders and relationships which... escape factual description. The factual language dissects and disintegrates experience into categories and oppositions that cannot be resolved. It is the language of either/or and from its standpoint all that is on the dark side of life—death, evil, and suffering—cannot be assimilated... By contrast, the language of myth and poetry is integrative, for the language of the image is *organic* language. Thus it expresses a point of view in which the dark side of things has its place, or rather, in which the light and the dark are transcended through being seen in terms of a dramatic unity. This is the catharsis or soul-cleansing function, of the tragic drama. [26]

It is significant, therefore, that Father Alesón gives him a book in Latin. Belarmino admits that he does not know Latin but, he says, «...Llegaré a tener intuición con él» (IV, 69). A book in Greek would have been as incomprehensible, but since Latin was, at one time, the universal language, Belarmino is really saying that he can gain a mystical intuition of the unity of the universe. This unity is composed of what factual language regards as opposites but which are really the same thing. For example, for Belarmino, the word «desnudar» signifies «Descubrir la verdad profunda, la causa». As a result, «desnudo» is «Causa última, explicación. ... El diablo desnudo es Dios». The dictionary that Escobar made of Belarmino's language shows several examples of the fact that, for Belarmino, language is organic. Thus «postema» signifies «sistema, tumor muerto en cuerpo vivo». (This would be an attack on the Neogrammarians.) Likewise, «sistema» is equivalent to «testarudez». «Paradoja» means «ortodoxia» with the implication that all absolutes are really paradoxical. The dictionary is called the cosmos but the word that Belarmino uses for «all» is the tetrahedron, a solid figure with four triangular faces. This word is interesting if one takes into consideration that three and four, and combinations thereof, have traditionally been considered mystic numbers. Perhaps tetrahedron could be the one all-encompassing word that Belarmino was searching for.

In his search for unity in language, Belarmino is the opposite of Father Alesón, whose nickname, «the Tower of Babel», refers to his «estatura y porque sabía veinte idiomas: unos vivos, otros muertos y otros putrefactos» (IV, 63). Not only is the Tower of Babel the very symbol of fragmentation in language, but Father Alesón's approach to language is the contrary of Belarmino's. Whereas Belarmino invents words and meanings, Father Alesón only imitates them. For this reason his magpie reminds Belarmino of the Dominican. For Father Alesón, language is a fixed body of rules which

---

[26] WATTS, pp. 15-16. We have already seen this version of the tragic drama in *Troteras y danzaderas*.

would place him among the Neogrammarians, whereas for Belarmino and the Neolinguists, language is forever changing:

> Father Alesón has a contractual view of language, which he sees as static by nature. Language for him is a set of useful conventions agreed upon by a particular society, and he has learned many languages to overcome the linguistic isolation of his fellow-men. Hence his nickname «Tower of Babel». He does not see language as an end in itself, as a worthy object of philosophical speculation, but as a means to an end... For [Belarmino]..., unlike Father Alesón, language is both a means and an end. [27]

Father Alesón is mainly preoccupied with communication, which stems from his gregarious nature. For this reason, he attempts to learn to speak like Belarmino in order to befriend him: «El padre Alesón hablaba ahora en este estilo conceptuoso y envuelto para dar por el gusto a Belarmino y granjearse su afecto» (IV, 105). Belarmino is happiest when he is alone with his «Inteleto», conjuring up camels and dromedaries out of his «cosmos». His daughter and Monsieur Colignon are the only ones with whom he wishes to maintain contact and, afraid that he will forget their language, he buys himself a magpie and teaches her poetry and oratory which are aspects of language that he despises but recognizes as necessary. Father Alesón learns Belarmino's language to win the cobbler's love; Belarmino makes an effort to remember his daughter's language because he loves her. The message seems to be that language is a combination of both invention and imitation, and that its ultimate purpose is to communicate love.

The plurality of meanings for each word in Belarmino's lexicon is not so unusual. Pérez de Ayala seems to feel that words are ambiguous anyway:

> Le digo a usted que cuando la duquesa soltaba un ajo, que en ella era signo de hallarse contenta, se quedaba uno embobado y sonriente como si escuchase una nota de ruiseñor. De las palabras no cuenta la estructura, sino el timbre y la intención; son como vasijas que, aunque de la misma forma, unas están hechas de barro y otras de cristal puro y contienen una esencia deliciosa. (IV, 77)

This ambiguity arises because each speaker uses words to accommodate personal needs:

> Cada una de esas palabras tiene en los diferentes filósofos un significado distinto y tal vez opuesto, y todo porque estos filósofos querían, lo mismo que usted, satisfacer las necesidades de su pensamiento. (IV, 127)

In summary, there are several dualistic aspects of language in this novel: authenticity versus inauthenticity in terms of self-expression and

[27] READ, p. 332.

self-knowledge, language as a static opposed to an organic phenomenon, words as reality in themselves or as ideal representations for the concrete thing, language as a unifying versus disintegrating factor and, finally, language as invention versus language as imitation. Indeed, the ambiguities inherent in language are perhaps the most important theme of *Belarmino y Apolonio.*

DUALISTIC PERSPECTIVES OF THE CHURCH

The Church plays an important role in this novel about the two cobblers. Although Pérez de Ayala still shows some anticlericalism, it is not as vitriolic as it was in *A.M.D.G.* His criticisms are not directed against priests so much as against the naive superstitious beliefs of some of the characters (notably the Neiras) and against the seminarians. Indeed his characterizations of both Guillén and Father Alesón, the two most important priests in the novel, are quite sympathetic, as is that of the bishop who defends his principles against the attack of the duchess:

> En medio de su contrariedad, la duquesa experimentaba una sensación aplaciente y alegre. «Esta visita —iba pensando al bajar las escaleras del palacio episcopal— me ha servido para apreciar mejor a Facundo. Es un hombre de voluntad y obra conforme a su conciencia... Antes le compadecía, ahora casi le admiro.» (IV, 150)

This mollified attitude is part of a generally more compassionate acceptance of differences by a more mature Pérez de Ayala. Nevertheless, the use of dualities is an inescapable aspect of the author's technique and in *Belarmino y Apolonio* there are several contrastive pairs that have to do with the Church:

1. The first pair of opposites is the *republicano* and the *sacerdote*. Don Celedonio de Obeso, «ateo declarado y republicano agresivo», and the priest don Guillén meet at the round table of doña Trina, the round table where we have already met the Limón sisters. When don Celedonio asks don Guillén if he believes in God, the priest retaliates by asking the other if he believes in the republic:

> —Como republicano que soy.
> —Yo, como sacerdote que soy, soy creyente. (IV, 24)

What has happened here is that Christianity and republicanism have become equivalent; they are both religions. Don Guillén emphasizes the interchangeability of Christianity and republicanism by stating that the early Christians started from the idea of God and arrived at the idea of the republic. Don Celedonio can therefore go back from the idea of the republic to the idea of God.

2. The opposition between the Church and the republic is again brought to mind in the description of the Rúa Ruera. The Círculo Republicano is situated next to the house of two rich priests and across the street from the episcopal palace.

3. The Church is put in opposition to the state: The state is a material community maintained by mutual convenience; the Church is a spiritual community sustained by mutual love. The state allows freedom of ideas but not of action; the Church allows freedom of action but is intransigent regarding ideas.

4. The Church is also contrasted with capitalism: Capitalism, a state of cruel and productive anarchy, is in contrast to the sweet, unproductive anarchy of the early Church. They are alike in that they are both anarchical.

5. The early Church was different from the later Church in that the former was a spiritual power and the latter a political force. This change is evident in the songs of the Breviary: Those of the early Church reflect simple faith; the songs from a later period mirror the power and glory of the Church. The early Church was inspired by love conceived in the heart; the later Church, by a love conceived in the head. In either case, the Church still symbolizes love.

6. In this regard, we also have the opposition between Pedro and Angustias: Pedro would represent the hypocrisy and power of the later Church; Angustias its earlier innocence. [28] Pedro is a priest, Angustias a prostitute. However, they do not conform to their expected roles:

> Although separated, they still form part of a whole, and the apparent contrastive doubles are not so different from one another as it would appear. Pedro seems... to show at times a worldliness incompatible with his profession... Angustias, on the other hand, is often compared to the Virgin. [29]

7. There are also two paradoxes that show that the spiritual world and the material world are inseparable: Father Alesón points out that he took a vow of poverty only to discover that, in so doing, he had become extremely rich. Wherever he might travel, he always has a home, usually very elegant, and plenty of food and money. This is one of the few really anticlerical assertions of the novel. The criticism of the Church's wealth is obvious, but it is couched in gentle humor by one of the novel's most likeable characters. The same humor is used to explain that believing is aided by not having to worry about material problems: «Para salvar el alma, lo más esencial es tener la mesa puesta a hora fija» (IV, 94).

[28] SARA SUÁREZ SOLÍS, Análisis de «Belarmino y Apolonio» (Oviedo: Instituto de Estudios Asturianos, 1974), p. 181.
[29] NEWBERRY, p. 59.

It is apparent that Pérez de Ayala has at least come to terms with the spirit of the Church, though not with its power. The spirit of the Church is love and it is significant that, when Belarmino and Apolonio speak to each other for the first time, «Belarmino se mantiene con los brazos en cruz» and Apolonio runs into them for the fraternal embrace.

DUALISMS WITHIN ONE PERSON

In the earlier novels one notes that, in spite of the fact that Pérez de Ayala uses many contrastive doubles, his characters tend to be unilateral; they are used in opposition to someone else, but are not contrastive within themselves. Although Rosina, for example, seems to have changed in *Troteras y danzaderas,* the change is only superficial for, in reality she has remained true to her pragmatic self. The two characters that have shown the most contradictory personalities are Teófilo Pajares and Arias Limón. In *Belarmino y Apolonio,* however, contradictions within the same person are of great importance and show a marked change in the author's technique. Juan Lirio asserts in his defense: «Pero concedo que me contradigo con frecuencia. ¿Y qué? Así me siento vivir» (IV, 36), and Pérez de Ayala uses these human contradictions to form the tragicomic elements that are so important in this novel.

The most common dualism found within a particular individual is sexual ambiguity, as exemplified by Perpetua Meana and doña Predestinación in the «novelas poemáticas». In the later novels, this dualism will become increasingly important. In *Belarmino y Apolonio,* one finds the following characters who incorporate both masculine and feminine qualities: Felicita Quemada is gracious and feminine from behind, but a front view reveals that she is flat-chested and masculine; there is a suspicion that Novillo is impotent because his nickname is «el Buey»; Father Alesón has a voice so high that his sigh «parecía más de monja que de fraile» (IV, 95); the Duchess of Somavia is feminine in appearance but masculine in words and actions; and, as already mentioned, Belarmino feels maternal love for his niece/daughter.

It seems almost impossible for Pérez de Ayala to describe a character without some contrastive element of personality. The following are examples of other contrasts within the same individual: don Celedonio; «ateo declarado y republicano agresivo, en el fondo un pedazo de pan, un zoquete» (IV, 23); Belarmino is a *zángano* to his wife and a saint to his daughter; Apolonio, although he would like to identify with his fighting cocks, is «incapaz de matar un mosquito...» (IV, 120); Novillo, an astute and daring politician, is, «en el fondo, la criatura más simple, candorosa, sentimental y asustadiza» (VI, 158); and Felicita: «alma jugosa y generosa como la vid buena, revestida de un tronco sarmentoso y casi momia» (IV, 179).

Finally, Sister Lucidia has a birthmark on the right side of her face. Consequently, her face seems to unite dark and light, night and day. The description of her age is also ambiguous: «Nada vieja; tampoco demasiado joven...» (IV, 203). In other words, not only in her face but also in her age she represents the union between life and death.

MISCELLANEOUS OPPOSITES

Belarmino y Apolonio has many minor contrastive doubles. Of particular interest are the following:

1. *The head versus the foot*

Special mention should be made of this dualism. Both Belarmino and Apolonio are very imaginative, yet they have both taken up shoemaking as a trade. For Belarmino, the answer lies in the fact that inventing new meanings for words is no different from stretching out shoes on his last. Apolonio explains that he chose to make shoes because they were first used in Greek drama to give height to the actors and make them appear more like gods. Moreover, he says, dramatic conflicts can only exist among men, and not among animals, precisely because man can stand straight and defy the heavens.

There has always been a traditional antagonism between intellectual effort and manual labor. Alfred Rodríguez says that in literature the tailors have competed with the shoemakers in showing this antagonism, but he thinks Pérez de Ayala chose shoemakers deliberately because «zapatero» has always been equivalent to «fracaso y torpeza» in Spanish folklore. The use of shoemakers would symbolize the failure of both drama and philosophy as means of knowing. [30] While not completely disagreeing, I find that Pérez de Ayala, in his usual manner, chose the most antithetical parts of the human body—the head and foot—to unite them in the persons of the two cobblers. Apolonio makes it very clear that the head and the foot are inseparable. Pedro says of him:

> Mi padre clasificaba a todas las personas que veía según ciertos rasgos de la fisonomía, y, cosa curiosa, del pie, y aseguraba: «Ese es noble», frente despejada, pie ario. «Ese es vil», sienes angostas, mandíbula prognata, pie planípedo, semita... (IV, 76)

The relation between head and foot is further emphasized when Belarmino is taken in by the Neiras. His *cuchitril* is below ground so that his head

---

[30] ALFRED RODRÍGUEZ, «Algo más sobre los zapateros de Pérez de Ayala», in *Simposio Internacional Ramón Pérez de Ayala, 1880-1980*, ed. Pelayo H. Fernández (Gijón: Imprenta Flores, 1981), p. 95.

is on the level of the passers-by on the street. Whereas Apolonio thinks that shoes, feet, and legs raise man up to the heavens, Belarmino is very happy to be below the ground:

> Belarmino pensaba hallarse providencialmente metido en la entraña de la tierra, colocado en la raíz y cimiento de las cosas, y que para conocer a los hombres lo mejor era verles nada más que los pies, que son la base y fundamento de las personas. (IV, 101)

This might be related to the Greek idea of the snake, a footless animal, wise because she can burrow into the heart of Mother Earth and learn her secrets.

2. *The magpie versus the fighting roosters*

Belarmino acquires a magpie who is like him in the somberness of her plumage; Apolonio owns fighting roosters who resemble him in their colorful strutting. Although the birds resemble their masters in their exterior appearance, they really symbolize a deep interior need in each man: Apolonio admires in the roosters their equanimity and bravery in the face of death. Keeping Socrates in mind, one might call this the «philosophical» attitude toward death and, hence, toward life. Belarmino, on the other hand, buys his magpie because he wants to keep in touch with the real world. He is aware that his «Inteleto» has him soaring at such heights that he is in danger of losing contact with his beloved daughter. This is but another example of the problem presented by don Amaranto in the Prologue—how to rise above and, at the same time, be submerged in the forest.

The birds are contrastive between themselves. The magpie, a member of the crow family, can be associated with death. Also, because the magpie collects things, one can make an association with the intellect. The rooster, on the other hand, has traditionally been associated with resurrection and, since these are fighting cocks, they represent action. In short, these birds symbolize that frequently-found dualism in Pérez de Ayala's novels: life versus death and action versus intellect.

3. *The laurel tree of the Prologue and the laurel trees of* Sub specie aeterni:

In ancient times, the laurel was the symbol for peace. When don Amaranto speaks of the laurel tree being disintegrated from its absolute unity by the scientists, he is implying that peace has also been fragmented. By contrast, the reunion of Belarmino and Apolonio under the laurel trees symbolizes victory over antagonism and restoration of peace.

4. *Tragedy and comedy*

The love affair between Felicita and Novillo, though pathetic to them, is comic to outsiders.

Apolonio considers his play a tragedy but Celemín converts it into a comic farce.

Novillo's death is tragic, but the author undermines the pathos by pointing out that his wig is on a bedpost and his teeth in a glass of water.

He uses the same technique with the Duchess by having her die with curling rags in her hair.

The fluctuation between comedy and tragedy is one of the most typical aspects of Ayala's techniques, especially in this novel:

> Lo cómico parece rondar siempre a lo heroico en el novelar de Pérez de Ayala, de acuerdo con su concepción de la tragicomedia... El que las cosas resulten serias o risibles no depende más que de un simple efecto de perspectiva...
>
> Mudada la perspectiva, con sólo un desplazamiento de la misma, una tragedia se convierte en farsa; el llanto se trueca en risa. [31]

5. *Other contrasts*

We find again the opposition between the northern lands of Asturias and the southern lands of Castile that appears in the earlier novels. In this instance, it occurs when the Duchess mentions that she hates Madrid because of its sun: «Le gustaban los cielos y la luz cernida. Decía que la luz de Madrid le alborotaba la sangre y la impulsaba a cometer barbaridades» (IV, 79), a statement reminiscent of *Insolación* by Pardo Bazán.

In this chapter, I have tried to point out all the dualistic possibilities in Pérez de Ayala's novel about the two shoemakers of Pilares. *Belarmino y Apolonio* is certainly his most perspectivistic work. The author seems to be making a deliberate effort to incorporate the ideas on perspectivism that Ortega y Gasset later elucidates in his *El tema de nuestro tiempo*. It seems, however, that what interests Pérez de Ayala most is not the multiplicity of viewpoints so much as the duality of opposing but similar forces. As a result of perspectivism, the clear-cut dualism that characterized the tetralogy has become progressively more polaristic in his later works. Opposites are no longer irreconcilable; they become poles joined by an axis. Moreover, the poles are often interchangeable, constantly shifting patterns and positions. What the author seeks now is the unifying force that holds these poles together. More and more, he will become preoccupied with unity:

---

[31] BAQUERO GOYANES, pp. 214-15.

Los dos son también síntesis de otra forma de desgarramiento de la personalidad que P de A sintetiza en estas palabras: «la lucha perpetua entre dos causas justas, la vital y la intelectual»... Apolonio es el vitalista; Belarmino, el intelectual y luego místico. También puede verse que Ap es conformista y Bel problemático, que Ap busca la catarsis y Bel la sofrosine. Pero éstas son diferencias y no afinidades, y nos demuestran la imposibilidad de fusionar en un solo personaje todos los valores humanos que suelen distribuirse en distintos seres y que P de A trata de condensar en dos, ya que no puede en uno. Es éste un problema que parece obsesivo en toda la obra de nuestro autor, especialmente en su última época. [32]

Marriage is the very symbol of unity in human existence. It seems appropriate, therefore, that the last two paired sets of novels by Pérez de Ayala are directed at the problem of marriage.

[32] SUÁREZ SOLÍS, p. 109.

5

LAS NOVELAS DE URBANO Y SIMONA

Pérez de Ayala divided his last two novels each into two parts. Andrés Amorós has chosen to call the first of these paired novels *Las novelas de Urbano y Simona* and I shall do the same. The decision to publish this novel in two parts seems to have been essentially an editorial one. It was felt that it would be too long if both parts were printed in one volume.[1] The first part bears the title *Luna de miel, luna de hiel* and the second *Los trabajos de Urbano y Simona*. Although the second part starts with a brief summary of the first, these two books really constitute one unified story.

Two Genres, Two Styles, Two Myths

Dualism is immediately obvious in the title of the first part, *Luna de miel, luna de hiel,* and a dualistic reference to the moon continues as a structural device: the first part is divided into «Cuarto menguante» and «Cuarto creciente», and the second into «Novilunio» and «Plenilunio». For Julio Matas and J. J. Macklin, the division of the novel into two parts shows a change in literary genres. Using Northrop Frye's definitions, Matas and Macklin feel that the first part is a tragedy and the second, a romance. The tragedy in part one is the result of a break with the normal pattern of nature, and hence the inversion of «Cuarto menguante» and «Cuarto creciente». Part two, however, ends happily with the restoration of normalcy in «Novilunio» and «Plenilunio».[2] Watts has said that «Evil is sensed pre-eminently... in what is strangely alien—not in sheer chaos and nonsense, but in profoundly odd and unnerving disturbances of the normal».[3] What has upset the normal pattern of life in *Luna de miel, luna de hiel* is a domineering mother

---

[1] Amorós, Introduction to *Honeymoon, Bittermoon,* by Ramón Pérez de Ayala, trans. Barry Eisenberg (Berkeley: University of California Press, 1972), p. xviii.
[2] Matas, p. 83.
[3] Watts, p. 37.

who has brought up her son, Urbano, in utter unawareness of the sexual facts of life. Urbano is married off to Simona because his mother wants social standing and Simona's wants wealth, but, because of the total ignorance of both young people, the honeymoon is disastrous. As don Cástulo, Urbano's teacher, says: «Hicimos de Urbano un ángel: esto es, un monstruo. Un ángel casado es un monstruo» (IV, 387). The marriage is not consummated, even though the young couple spend a week together (in separate bedrooms) in an idyllic setting which is where they truly begin their courtship, and Urbano begins to realize that there is something important that he does not know. Thus the normal pattern of sexual awareness first, then courtship, and finally marriage has been reversed; Urbano and Simona get married, then have a courtship and, in the second book, finally become sexually aware.[4] The awareness that occurs in the second part in turn begins a normal pattern: Urbano decides to court his wife and win her for his own, and they are finally able to have a real honeymoon. The break with the normal pattern of nature, the sense of foreboding, and «the recurrent mentions of fate in the opening pages», as well as Urbano's «recognition of his tragic weakness», and the novel's catastrophic end all help to place *Luna de miel* within the genre of the tragedy.[5]

Los trabajos de Urbano y Simona, on the other hand, is a romance in which Urbano becomes a chivalric hero whose quest is winning Simona's love. He must overcome great obstacles and experience many adventures in the style of the «comedias de capa y espada» before he can finally succeed. His character has changed, however; he has become a man and he is master of his own fate:

> Esta voluntad de Urbano de ser, «y no el designio ajeno, el hacedor de su propia historia», es la cualidad de su carácter que interesa a Ayala destacar en «Plenilunio»; por ello, decide convertirlo en un héroe de aventuras con algo de fabuloso, libérrimo creador de su destino, como antes había hecho de él un héroe trágico, a la merced del hado o de la voluntad de otros.[6]

Nevertheless, although the first part is a tragedy and the second a romance, the two are complementary in that almost everything in the second part is a direct reversal of the first. The first part ends in catastrophe; the second ends happily. The second is a step-by-step correction of the errors committed in the first,[7] and in the end the young lovers come back full circle to where they had started, although much changed and now truly ready to have their «luna de miel».

[4] MATAS, p. 84.
[5] J. J. MACKLIN, «Romance and Realism: Pérez de Ayala's Urbano and Simona Novels», *Neophilologus,* 64, No. 2 (April 1980), 217.
[6] MATAS, p. 102.
[7] MATAS, p. 85.

In addition to two genres, there is also the confrontation between two artistic styles, two ways of looking at the world: the classical and the romantic. The one conscious of this confrontation is don Cástulo, a man learned in the classical literatures and who has always abhorred the romantics:

> ¿En qué iba a parar una educación disparatada, ilógica, contra todos los principios de la pedagogía clásica y los dictados del sentido común, sino en este paso en que lo bufo se mezcla con lo patético como en los dramas románticos? Pero yo no transijo con el romanticismo y sus géneros híbridos. Yo no soy un romántico. Yo soy un clásico. Yo quiero cosas claras, géneros definidos, situaciones inteligibles... Si bien..., ¿estás seguro, pobre Cástulo, de no ser un romántico? (IV, 280-81)

The irony is that, time and again, Cástulo behaves exactly like the most stereotyped romantic hero: «Señora, soy un amante desgraciado — suspiró con oquedad de ultratumba, las cejas unidas en acento circunflejo y llevándose una mano sobre el corazón» (IV, 291). In the end, he realizes that life cannot be divided into categories: «—¿Egloga o tragedia? Nada, que me entrego. Converso soy al romanticismo. El amor es una cosa trágica y grotesca de consuno. Sin duda hay géneros literarios híbridos como hay animales híbridos y personas híbridas» (IV, 293-94).

Not only does the novel represent two genres and two styles, it is also based on two myths: the pagan story of Daphnis and Chloe and the Judeo-Christian myth of Adam and Eve. Moreover, these two myths are so fused that they become inseparable. The pastoral setting of Simona's farm, where the innocent young couple spend the first week of their marriage, is frequently compared to Paradise, but Urbano soon senses that they must be evicted from this paradise because of his thirst for knowledge. Moreover, although still sexually unaware, his innocent cavorting with Simona has made him aware of her body and, in his mind's eye, he has seen the two of them naked. Like Daphnis and Chloe, the two have become increasingly frustrated sexually, although they themselves do not understand it. Urbano, however, begins to ask questions and therefore he is not surprised when the «punishment» comes and they are expelled from the farm. But, as Simona's grandmother doña Rosita points out, this is a false paradise:

> El mundo, hijos míos, se muere de aburrimiento. Es preferible la aflicción al tedio. En vuestras próximas y terribles aflicciones... emborrachaos como en una batalla, y luego alegraos con frenesí, como salvajes victoriosos. Que nada os amilane... Acercaos a la ventana, los dos juntos. Mirad el jardín, el parque. ¿Diréis que es el Paraíso perdido? No, sino el limbo. Y si para vosotros fue Paraíso, que sí lo fue, débese a vuestras congojas y anhelo de dicha, que no habéis logrado. El paraíso está fuera, más allá de esos muros, en las luchas de la vida. (IV, 367)

The paradox is obvious: the pastoral innocence of Daphnis and Chloe or of Adam and Eve would, in the end, be boring. The «sin» of knowledge, with its subsequent trials and tribulations, is what gives value to life. And, in order to become mature individuals who can take their rightful place in society, Urbano and Simona must leave the idyllic countryside and go back to civilization, back to the city.

NATURE VERSUS CULTURE

Although the theme of culture versus nature is ancient in literature, it seems that Pérez de Ayala uses it in a consciously dualistic manner. Pelayo H. Fernández has studied the definitions our author gives to certain terms:

Civilización

> Una ciudad se gobierna a sí misma. Mejor dicho, el gobierno, en su forma más esquemática, nace con la ciudad...
> Una nación *civilizada* es aquella en que está resuelto el problema político y cuyos ciudadanos gozan de libertad de espíritu y robustez de voluntad. [8]

In light of his concepts of civilization, it is easy to see why Ayala chose to name his protagonist Urbano. Urbano has lived all his life in the city, so much so that he cannot tell the difference between a bull and a cow. He received the education necessary to obtain a lawyer's degree, but it was a learning process carefully controlled by his mother in which any references to the facts of life were literally cut out of his books. He has memorized the lessons like a parrot, under the tutelage of don Cástulo, never questioning the foundations of what he memorized and his degrees were bought with bribes by his father. In other words, it was no education at all. In the second book, however, Urbano sets out to educate himself, whereupon he becomes a truly «civilized» person. He learns to govern himself instead of being governed by his mother, and he uses his own will to achieve the spiritual freedom he perceives is necessary to become a mature man.

The polar opposite of Urbano is Simona, the representative of nature. She has lived all her life on the farm and she introduces Urbano to the rustic beauty of her domains. The difference between them, the man bound by the rules of society and the free-spirited country girl, is clearly shown in the following passage:

---

[8] FERNÁNDEZ, *Ideario etimológico de Ramón Pérez de Ayala* (Madrid: José Porrúa Turanzas, 1982), pp. 54 and 56.

> Despúes del desayuno, Simona propuso a su natural amo y señor salir
> juntos y conducirle a visitar la vasta finca.
> —Voy por el sombrero —dijo Urbano.
> —¿Sombrero, para qué, si estamos dentro de nuestra casa? —opinó Simona,
> tomando al marido de la mano y arrastrándole al jardín. (IV, 300)

In the end, Urbano understands that intellectual learning must necessarily
be joined to nature because man has lost his animal instincts; man must
be taught not only to eat but also to procreate.

The problem of education versus nature is discussed at length by don
Cástulo and doña Rosita. The latter expounds the traditional view that
civilization is the control of nature by man:

> A mí, desde niña, me enseñaron que la educación consiste precisamente en
> oponerse, y cuando no, en sobreponerse a la Naturaleza. Naturaleza son los
> rayos del cielo, las tormentas del mar, los temblores de la tierra, las lluvias
> torrenciales, el hielo que atenaza y el calor que ahoga. Apañados estábamos si
> en todos estos casos dejásemos obrar a la Naturaleza, sin combatirla o al me-
> nos defendernos de ella. Seres de naturaleza son las bestias: vacas y toros,
> yeguas y caballos, ovejas y carneros, gallinas y gallos, que de todo hay con
> abundancia en esta finca. ¿Qué propone usté, amigo mío: que Simona y Ur-
> bano se instruyan en el amor mediante los ejemplos que, sin transponer siquiera
> los muros de nuestra posesión, les proporcionen las bestias?
> —Tanto como eso...
> —No, es que ni con eso se instruirán, porque son inocentes, y sólo los ojos
> torpes aciertan a ver las cosas torpes. (IV, 286)

Doña Rosita is right. Urbano and Simona do not understand the natural
events that surround them, something that is perhaps understandable in
Urbano, since he had lived his whole life in the city in a very protected
environment, but is harder to accept in Simona. One would suspect she
had at least known about eggs being laid, even if she had not seen calves
being born. Nevertheless, Pérez de Ayala never meant to write a realistic
story. In fact, J. J. Macklin may be right when he says:

> We can see then that the Greek romances... attracted Ayala because of
> certain literary problems they raised. Their essential eclecticism offers a model
> for the modern non-Realist writer who wishes to dramatise the actual creative
> process itself, to dramatise, indeed, the conflict between artistic rules and ar-
> tistic pleasure and freedom. [9]

The same can be said of the biological creative process. The conflict between the rules of society and natural pleasure and freedom is one of
the themes of this novel. Ayala will explore this subject again in *Tigre
Juan,* especially with regard to the young Colás, and he seems to conclude
that there should be a happy compromise between the two, with the edge

---

[9] MACKLIN, «Romance and Realism», pp. 224-25.

perhaps given to nature. It is significant that Urbano says: «Primero, me creo una posición firme; en seguida, robo a Simona. Así, robada. Ni sacramento ni contrato. Nuestro amor es una cosa única en el mundo y, por lo tanto, está por fuera y por cima de la ley» (IV, 510), an idea which will be taken up in *Tigre Juan* by doña Iluminada.

The person who, because of his learning, is the most conscious of the absurdities of the situation is don Cástulo. He very quickly comes to the conclusion that the «good» education he had helped give Urbano is absurd because it is contrary to nature, and he now proposes to give Urbano «la mala educación», an idea which quite startles doña Rosita:

> —Su teoría, por lo que me ha declarado, incluye en el tratado de la buena educación un capítulo donde se instruya e incite a la mala educación...
> —Ha hablado usté de la digestión; que se debe enseñar a digerir; y ha insinuado que se debería enseñar a amar; amar en el sentido material.
> —Sí, señora; pero eso no sería mala educación, sino buena educación.
> —Perfectamente; a eso iba. A mí, desde niña, me habían enseñado que todo lo que no se puede hacer en presencia de los demás cae bajo lo que comúnmente se llama mala educación. Pero usté añade que a estas cosas de la vieja mala educación hay que someterlas también a una buena educación. ¡Donoso descubrimiento! Sí, señor; me ilumina usté. Nunca se me había ocurrido. (IV, 292)

The dualistic opposites civilization versus nature and «la buena educación» versus «la mala educación» lead to the conclusion that the completely fulfilled man must join the two.

Some additional opposites demonstrate the antithesis of civilization and nature:

1. When the two officials come to tell doña Rosita that she must leave her farm, the maid announces them as «dos hombres», whereupon doña Rosita corrects her:

> —¿Dos hombres? —preguntó doña Rosita, arrugando las narices con voluntaria comicidad—. ¿Dos hombres, nada menos, para mí sola?
> —Dos hombres, o dos señores, como quiera la señora, sola o acompañada.
> —No es lo mismo hombres que señores. (IV, 354)

2. When doña Rosita is dying, she asks Simona to get her wedding dress out of the trunk. Wrapped in tissue paper are two flowers. One, a rose which her «capitán de fragata» gave her on the day of their first kiss, is now nothing but dust; the other, an orange blossom, is still in perfect condition:

> —Dame ahora ese paquetito de papel de seda que está sobre la mesa. Acércate bien. Mira. Esto que parece polvo es una rosa. La rosa que me dio el día del primer beso. ¿Ves? Polvo... Mira esto otro, entre el polvo; la flor

de azahar, símbolo del matrimonio puro, de la unión entre dos como es debido. Mira esta flor; está como el primer día. El amor, el amor loco, pasó. Esto permanece... Y esta flor siempre estará lo mismo, en tanto pasan las generaciones de rosas. (IV, 381-82)

This passage from the end of book one is repeated at the conclusion of book two where Simona shows the dust and the orange blossom to Urbano and quotes her grandmother's words. Urbano, however, is quick to see that the orange blossom is artificial and says:

—No te enternezcas, Simona. Ten en cuenta... que esta flor de azahar es de cera, falsificada por los hombres, obra industrial. Y la rosa era una rosa viva, una rosa de fuego; por eso es ahora cenizas. Y nosotros no somos figuras de cera; somos dos llamas de la misma hoguera. Antes de apagarnos habremos transmitido a otros la antorcha encendida. (IV, 546)

Pérez de Ayala is implying that the rules regarding chastity in marriage, represented by the orange blossom, are fixed because they are ideas conceived by man as necessary for the good of society. However, they do not depict true love, a natural impulse symbolized by the rose which, because it is natural, is mortal. It would be against nature to live forever; they will love, they will die, but they will have passed the fire of life on to others.

3. Again the contrast between nature and society is evident when don Cástulo tells Conchona that he wants to ask her father for her hand in marriage, an idea that seems strange to her:

Conchona no entendió qué era aquello de pedir algo a sus padres. Que no les pidiese nada, porque nada tenían; y aun cuando lo tuviesen, no lo darían. Era pedirla en matrimonio, pedir el consentimiento paterno, elucidó don Cástulo. Esto lo entendía menos Conchona. Ella era quien tenía que consentir, y ya había consentido... Aun así y todo, don Cástulo no quería omitir aquella solemnidad ceremoniosa. (IV, 434)

4. It is significant that doña Micaela, upon realizing the error of her ways, should want to change her «vestidos de señora» for «las prendas plebeyas». She takes off her corset not only to attract the husband she has rejected for years, but also to be acquiescent to a nature which, by sheer force of will, she had insisted on changing.

5. Finally, Conchona does not understand the word «prostitution». «Cuando oía lo de prostitución, Conchona creía que se iban a enzarzar en una polémica política como otras tardes. A ella, prostitución y constitución le sonaban lo mismo. Retirábase porque le aburría aquel tema» (IV, 525). Conchona symbolizes the Earth Mother, nature in her most open, generous self. Prostitution sells love for gold and, if gold and commerce are the basis for civilization, the inference seems to be that prostitution is a product of civilization and therefore contrary to nature.

Nature pitted against civilization is one of the basic dualisms in *Las novelas de Urbano y Simona*. The message that comes across most clearly, however, is that they should not be considered opposites but, rather, two poles, both necessary for man's well-being. Pérez de Ayala is emphasizing very much the same idea as Ortega y Gasset in *El tema de nuestro tiempo*:

> Durante siglos se viene hablando exclusivamente de la necesidad que la vida tiene de la cultura. Sin desvirtuar lo más mínimo esta necesidad, se sostiene aquí que la cultura no necesita menos de la vida. Ambos poderes —el inmanente de lo biológico y el trascendente de la cultura— quedan de esta suerte cara a cara, con iguales títulos, sin supeditación del uno al otro. [10]

MALE VERSUS FEMALE

In the opinion of Guillermo Díaz-Plaja, all dualisms start with the basic biological dualism of male and female: «El punto de partida sería la realidad biológica. El Varón y la Mujer, como dual inicio universal de toda historia posible, como clave última de toda actitud mental en el tiempo y en el espacio.» [11] The ideal in marriage is to bring together male and female so that the two fuse into one, both physically and spiritually. *Las novelas de Urbano y Simona* explore the possibilities of such a union, a union often impeded by the restrictions of a misguided society. As a result, the male and female dualism becomes the basic theme and everything else is subordinate to it. However, since more emphasis is given to Urbano's feelings and reactions, the feminine viewpoint is not always as well developed.

Díaz-Plaja summarizes the dualistic alternations posited by a contemporary of Ayala, Eugenio d'Ors, [12] of which the following are of special interest: «Cultura» (the city and Athens) is given as masculine; «Natura» (the forests and Demeter) as feminine. As I said, Urbano represents civilization and Simona, nature.

Logos is masculine; its opposite is Pan. When doña Rosita falls in a faint upon hearing that she will lose her farm, a primeval scream erupts from Simona:

> Oyóse el alarido de la tragedia cuando la miserable palabra humana, tan inexpresiva para todo lo que es supremo, se anula y el grito brota; ese alarido que amedrenta la carne mortal con más eficacia que el mismo espectáculo de la muerte. Era Simona, que se arrojaba sobre el cuerpo yacente de la abuela. (IV, 357-58)

---

[10] ORTEGA Y GASSET, pp. 143-44.
[11] GUILLERMO DÍAZ-PLAJA, *Modernismo frente a Noventa y Ocho* (Madrid: Espasa-Calpe, 1951), p. 200.
[12] DÍAZ-PLAJA, p. 209.

Urbano, on the other hand, remains impassive to the scene before him:

> Urbano permanecía quieto, impasible, las manos en los bolsillos, atento a las circunstancias con que se desarrollaba la catástrofe. Lo había oído y visto todo con una especie de curiosidad intelectual. Lo único que le interesaba era la forma que adoptaban los sucesos, puesto que del desenlace estaba prevenido de antemano. Sabía que les iban a arrojar del Paraíso. (IV, 358)

Doña Rosita, however, is able to perceive the polaristic paradox when she recovers from her faint:

> Tú, Urbano, que estás al parecer tranquilo, eres el más desconcertado. Tú, Simona, tan descompuesta en tus facciones, no has perdido el asiento y firmeza del alma. Estás desconcertado, Urbano, porque piensas en el porvenir. Estás firme, Simona, porque, con el sobresalto del momento, no sospechas que hay un mañana. (IV, 365)

This idea brings forward the concept of a male and female history. D'Ors puts «Historia» in the masculine realm and «Prehistoria» in the feminine. I prefer the ideas of Spengler which, as summarized by Díaz-Plaja, sound quite close to Unamuno's idea of *intrahistoria*:

> El hombre hace la historia; la mujer *es* la historia. De manera misteriosa descúbrese aquí un doble sentido del acontecer viviente: es una corriente cósmica y es también la sucesión de los microcosmos mismos que aquella corriente acoge en sí, protege y conserva. Esta «segunda» historia es la propiamente masculina, la historia política y social... Femenina es aquella «primera» historia, la historia eterna, materna, vegetal..., *la historia sin cultura de las generaciones sucesivas,* que no cambia... [13]

It is significant that doña Rosita wears a pendant which holds a small portrait. Don Leoncio thinks it is Rosita herself or possibly Simona but, as it turns out, it is a portrait of Rosita's grandmother. This portrait, therefore, seems to represent the generations of women, unchanging and eternal, who make up the *intrahistoria* upon which men build their *historia*. Therefore Urbano can say, «No hay un ayer. Sólo hay un mañana. Y el mañana se llama *Simona de carne y hueso*» (IV, 445), whereupon he sets out to be «el hacedor de su propia historia. En el atrio del futuro escribía alegremente: *Incipit*» (IV, 448). And, near the end of his educational process, Urbano comes to this conclusion about male and female roles in history:

> La mujer forma, con su propia carne y con su propia sangre, el cuerpo vivo de la Humanidad, misión en que el hombre toma una parte mezquina, instantánea y desdeñable. Por esto mismo, que es decreto de la Naturaleza, el hombre se ve libre y desocupado a lo largo de la vida, para idear, para luchar, para crear; en suma, para pensar, inventar la historia. (IV, 528)

[13] Díaz-Plaja, p. 207.

Another division made by d'Ors is that «Realidad» is masculine, and «Sueño» feminine. Again one can find a corollary to this idea in *Luna de miel*:

> Porque así como para Simona, bajo el influjo de Urbano, el mundo exterior cesaba de existir por instantes, para Urbano, bajo el influjo de Simona, la realidad de las cosas y la realidad de su propio cuerpo y de su espíritu se despertaba por instantes de la nada nebulosa que era su anterior estado, la de él y la del universo. (IV, 304)

The «realidad» of Urbano and the «sueño» of Simona are both brought out by the nearness of the other; in other words, Simona brings out in Urbano his masculine qualities, and vice versa.

Again according to d'Ors, the exterior, visual world falls within the masculine realm, while the interior, auditive world is feminine. (The name Simon-Simona comes from a Hebrew word meaning «to hearken».) This time, instead of evincing his masculine traits, Urbano, as a result of his communion with Simona, acquires some traits of the feminine realm —namely, he learns to hear:

> Domingo a la mañana. Urbano probó una sensación nueva; oyó campanas por primera vez...
> Tañeron las campanas de la iglesia. Por la diafanidad y sosiego de la atmósfera, sonaban como junto al oído. La vibración metálica se propagó por la carne de Urbano, enterneciéndole. Dijo a Simona:
> —Calcula si habré oído campanas infinitas veces; pues en verdad te digo que no las había oído hasta ahora. (IV, 303-04)

Urbano becomes more of a man as the novel progresses, but part of the process seems to be to allow his feminine side to develop as well.

D'Ors puts Classicism within the masculine realm, and Romanticism within the feminine. Urbano was given a classical education. Simona, on the other hand, is the ideal romantic heroine, a pure and innocent child of nature who inspires Urbano to become a superior being. She is like Goethe's «eternal feminine» ideal.

In addition, there are other aspects of the male/female relationship explored in *Las novelas de Urbano y Simona*. A great part of the novel is devoted to analyzing the reactions of men and women to love and marriage. For example, when Urbano begins to fall in love with Simona, the world becomes alive for him:

> Jamás se había sentido tan feliz, y su felicidad era como una intuición de crecimiento... Con Simona, se gozaba no tanto en su vecindad y hermosura cuanto en sentirse vivir él mismo, con abandono y plétora, casi en sentirse nacer a la vida y a la luz. (IV, 301)

For Simona, on the contrary, the world recedes into the background, and only Urbano exists. At the end of the novel, Urbano has become a mature man with a better understanding of the male and female roles in life:

> Obcecados y sin albedrío, desafiando a la muerte, los humanos corren hacia el amor, que no es sino el triunfo y la superación de la vida sobre la muerte. Fatalmente, el hombre gravita hacia la mujer y la mujer atrae al hombre, y no hay obstáculo que se interponga. Y no sólo la Humanidad, sino la Naturaleza entera está repartida en dos elementos: el eterno femenino, que atrae, y el eterno masculino, que es atraído inevitablemente... El universo se le representaba una lucha infinita y absoluta de sexos, como girando sobre un eje, cuyos dos polos fuesen lo masculino y lo femenino, lo que es atraído y lo que atrae, lo que engendra y lo que concibe. Todas las viejas teogonías imaginaban asimismo el universo girando sobre dos polos fijos, el bien y el mal absolutos, Ormuzd y Ahrimán. Según eso, ¿sería cada uno de los sexos un ideal de bien absoluto y un germen de mal absoluto? ¿Cuál sería el bien? ¿Lo masculino? No, no hay bien ni mal absolutos; hay bienes y males relativos, en la medida que cada uno de los elementos, el masculino y el femenino, cumplen su finalidad o la contrarían. (IV, 527-28)

The whole novel is an extensive analysis of the most basic of dualistic opposites, the male and the female, which Pérez de Ayala sees as the two poles of the universe.

Urbano comes to the realization that the female role is to attract, a role which Simona, in her innocence, is aware of instinctively. Since Urbano does not court her in the beginning, she courts him:

> Era otra Simona. Habiendo abdicado Urbano de la iniciativa amorosa, que por naturaleza corresponde al varón, Simona, bajo el imperativo de la especie, tomaba la iniciativa. Sin designio, con inocencia perfecta, sintiéndose turbada en todas sus fibras al contacto con Urbano, púdicamente y como al acaso, le rozaba las manos, la frente, los ojos, las mejillas, la boca, a pretexto de azotarle con una flor... (IV, 316-17)

This incident takes place in *Luna de miel.* In *Los trabajos,* however, it is Urbano who takes the initiative and Simona becomes the prototype of the captive princess, passively awaiting rescue by her knight. Thus, normalcy is restored in the second book.[14] In fact, the masculine/feminine roles are given further emphasis by the fact that Urbano kidnaps Simona from a convent, an act which brings to mind Don Juan, the prototype of the aggressive male.

DUALISMS WITHIN ONE PERSON

The male/female opposition just studied is embodied within two persons, man and woman. We still need to examine the dualisms that can

[14] MATAS, p. 99.

exist within the same person, a trait that is very typical of Pérez de Aya-la's character portrayals.

The most noticeable dualism within the same person is the androgynous. One notes the following examples:

Doña Micaela, Urbano's mother, is the outstanding character of this type. Although a woman, she has the iron will usually attributed to the male, a will so strong that she changes reality to suit her ends:

> Doña Micaela... no admitía la realidad tal cual espontáneamente se ofrece, sino que, antes de aceptarla, pretendía convertirla en lo que ella, doña Micaela, quería que fuese y creía que debía ser. En lugar de someterse a la realidad, la sometía. (IV, 235)

Micaela wishes that she were a man and Urbano's birth fulfills her wish: «Ya soy hombre; mi hijo soy yo misma; haré de él lo que apetezca. Aquí tengo la vida, la vida ciega, que puede ser maldad y dolor, o bondad y dicha, sujeta a mi arbitrio» (IV, 244-45). She makes herself masculine in appearance as well as in temperament:

> La propia Micaela se apañaba escrupulosamente para anular la traza externa del sexo con ropajes austeros, casi sacerdotales, el peinado liso y unos justillos o coseletes que le dejaban raso el pecho. Hasta había adquirido catadura masculina. (IV, 457)

Nevertheless, when her husband, don Leoncio, goes bankrupt, the domineering doña Micaela undergoes an abrupt psychological reversal and now becomes his adoring slave. Whereas before she had rejected her husband, she now makes amorous advances toward him and even dreams of having another child, a girl. Before, she had used her determination to reach wealth and social position; now she is determined to enjoy being poor. In other words, she has exchanged her masculine role for a more feminine one, but she is still the same strong-willed Micaela:

> Don Cástulo analizaba mentalmente la situación, separando sus elementos. «Elemento primordial, fuerza que domina todas las demás: doña Micaela. Mujer extraordinaria. Rectilínea, dominante, ambiciosa. Salida de la nada, quiso encumbrarse. Subió, subió, seguro el paso, la cabeza firme, sin mirar atrás. Ya tenía un pie en la cumbre. Se creía rica... De repente, todo se derrumba, y ella rueda hacia el fondo. Pero cae con el mismo coraje y ferocidad con que antes se elevaba. Criatura de una pieza, esculpida en materia tenaz; no se dobla ni se rompe; nunca estará oblicua, nunca estará curva; se la volverá de arriba abajo y permanecerá perpendicular...» (IV, 387)

However, in the second book, doña Micaela goes mad. Thomas Feeney has said that «Micaela will be one of his few characters not to gain Ayala's compassion» [15] because she denied her feminine role. I disagree. It

---

[15] THOMAS FEENY, «Maternal-Paternal Attitudes in the Fiction of Ramón Pérez de Ayala». *Hispanófila*, 62 (1978), 79.

seems, rather, that Pérez de Ayala makes her undergo a pathetic madness in order to attract the reader's sympathy, thereby corroborating his idea that no one is completely evil. And Micaela was a dedicated mother, wanting only the best for her son. The author is very careful to explain that her childhood experiences form the basis of her aversion to sex and her despotic will to power. In short, Doña Micaela «es otro de los grandes personajes femeninos creados por Ayala». [16]

Another androgynous character is don Cástulo, «varón conspicuo por su mansedumbre...» (IV, 226). Traditionally, *mansedumbre* is a feminine virtue, admirable in the woman but not in the man. Of small physique and timid nature, he is not surprised when doña Micaela, in her lucid madness, asks who his husband is:

> —Dispénsame que no te lo haya dicho de antemano... Estoy casado.
> —¡Ah, sí! Se me olvidaba. ¿Y quién es tu marido?
> —¿Cómo mi marido? Dirás mi mujer, Micaela.
> —No digo tu mujer, sino tu marido.
> Don Cástulo guardó silencio. Le dio un vuelco el corazón. Siempre había sido sincero y valeroso para consigo mismo en sus cogitaciones y exámenes de conciencia (en lo único en que no era cobarde). Pensó ahora: «Mujer excepcional; hasta en su locura y sinrazón la inspira un soplo adivinatorio. Mirándolo bien, ¿no es Conchita el marido y yo la mujer?» Por no contrariar a doña Micaela, respondió don Cástulo:
> —Mi marida, Micaela, es un hombre casi perfecto. (IV, 478)

Doña Micaela then asks of him: «¿Vas tú a parir, Cástulo? ¿Cuándo pares?»:

> —Dentro de ocho meses —respondió don Cástulo, desfallecido, con imperceptible aliento.
> ¡Oh, Dios! Aquella secreta emoción de llegar a ser padre, que él conceptuaba como la más sublime..., bien poca cosa era comparada con la emoción continua, creciente, entrañable, abrumadora y dolorosa en que la madre está totalmente absorbida el largo lapso desde que concibe hasta que da a luz el hijo. Esto se lo había hecho sentir, más que comprender, doña Micaela, por virtud de su aberración cerebral, ahora, en una especie de sugestión física. (IV, 478-79)

There are several characters in Pérez de Ayala's novels who combine maternal and paternal roles. [17] I have already commented that Belarmino's feelings for his niece were quite maternal. Doña Micaela is the «father» of the family (she sits at the head of the table). This combination will become fully harmonious in the personality of Tigre Juan who not only

---

[16] ENRIQUE JUNCEDA AVELLO, «La mujer en la obra de Pérez de Ayala», in *Pérez de Ayala visto en su centenario, 1880-1980* (Oviedo: Instituto de Estudios Asturianos, 1981), p. 210.
[17] See article by THOMAS FEENY.

feels within his own body his wife's gestation (like Cástulo) but also suffers her birth pangs.

Don Cástulo dreams he is being abducted by a superb Amazon, a dream which later becomes true. His Amazon is Conchona, also an androgynous character, who is his complementary opposite in many ways. He is thin and small, she is amply endowed; he is cerebral, she is spontaneous; he is bashful, she is aggressive and does the courting; he is idealistic and given to theorizing, she is realistic and practical. Conchona has many masculine qualities, in spite of her motherly and fecund feminity. It is Conchona, with her «coraje viril», who protects doña Rosita's farm from the thieving servants, much as doña Predestinación protected Cástor and Balbina from the mockers:

> Yo sola me basto contra todos vosotros, que, aunque mujer, tengo pelos en la cara. Al que se desmande, por los huesos de mis defuntos que lo mato de un tiro o le afondo en la panza los dientes de este chuzo envenenado.
> Nadie rechistó entre la sorpresa y el miedo. ... La Conchona, sin dignarse mirar, prosiguió triunfante, endiosada, la lanza en alto. Don Cástulo la hubiera comparado con Palas Atenea. En su virilismo arrogante, estaba casi hermosa. (IV, 379)

Urbano himself is a mixture of masculine and feminine traits:

> Por fin..., el unigénito: ... mancebo de veinte años, voluminoso de cabeza, fisonomía en exceso aniñada para la edad, bigotejo primerizo, tez lechosa como de fruta madurecida en el sobrado; muy tímido, exageradamente susceptible al rubor y aun al llanto, y como contraste, mandíbula ancha, que denotaba fuerte voluntad, acaso soterrana y en germinación todavía. (IV, 226)

Both don Cástulo and Simona describe him as «un ángel» — angels, it must be remembered, are sexless. Finally, when doña Micaela goes mad, she thinks he is her imaginary daughter Ángeles.

Even Simona is given attributes of the opposite sex. When she is sick and has to have her hair cut off, she looks like a young boy, and the fact that she has lost weight adds to the illusion: «La cabeza, cubierta de menudos bucles cincelados en cobre, y el exangüe rostro de alabastro parecían pertenecer a un bello adolescente; más delgada, en el grácil torso no se insinuaban protuberancias femeninas» (IV, 543).

In addition to the androgynous dualism found within the same person, there is the parent/child relationship. The characters in *Las novelas de Urbano y Simona* are constantly changing these roles.

The description of Urbano given above is at the beginning of *Luna de miel* when he is still an adolescent. However, his strong jaw indicates the determination that will eventually make him a man. As he progresses toward manhood, his relationship with his mother begins to change, and as she goes mad, she becomes more and more like a child to him:

All resentment of past injuries vanishes as Urbano watches his mother's grasp on reality steadily loosen. Like Leoncio he, too, now regards her paternally. Recalling his earlier thought that Micaela had never been a child, Urbano kisses her, murmuring: «'Esta es mi niñita, mi niñita querida'»... But with a touch of grotesque humor, Ayala immediately moves to keep the relationship pattern unstable. Micaela laughs that Urbano should call her «niña», for in her madness she believes him to be a non-existent daughter named Ángeles; reproaching her son, Micaela cries scornfully: «'¡Ah, tontuela! ¡Niña me dices! La niña eres tú.'» [18]

There is the implication, nevertheless, that Urbano, in spite of his desire to become a man, has a contrary impulse to remain a child. When he first discovers the truth about sexual relations in marriage, his first instinct is to run to his mother for protection:

Abrióse la puertecilla. Apareció Urbano, que se arrojó a abrazarse con su madre, estrujándola contra sí entre sollozos convulsivos.
—¡Mamá! ¡Mamá! ¡Madre! ¡Madre mía! —balbucía Urbano, y su acento era como el de los adioses eternos.
—Ea, ea; reprímete, Urbano. No más chiquilladas. Ya eres un hombre —amonestó la madre con austeridad.
—No quiero ser hombre. Que me devuelvan mi niñez —gritó desolado el mozo. (IV, 411)

Within marriage, also, the partners can leave the traditional husband-wife role and become a parent to each other. Don Leoncio and doña Micaela's changing relationship clearly shows this:

Ironically, her husband, not her son, first arouses the maternal instinct in Micaela. When Leoncio's business fails, as solace for his woes she offers him sex. But long denied the role of husband to Micaela, Leoncio has gradually assumed that of parent to her; finding abhorrent the idea of sexual relations with one whom he now regards as his child, Leoncio can love his wife only «como un padre quiere a un hijo descastado e insolente»... When she becomes totally mad, Micaela no longer presses for conjugal affections but now, in her vulnerability, accepts the role of child. Leoncio at last is able to express physically his paternal tenderness toward her: «Ahora sí que podía estrechar y besar a Micaela como a una niña adorada y doliente...» [19]

In like manner, both Simona and Conchona have maternal attitudes toward their husbands:

At length the image of Simona's body awakens his dormant sexual instincts; ... Simona finally fulfills the maternal task and brings her husband to manhood: «Tú me has hecho hombre, Simona»..., he tells her repeatedly. [20]

[18] FEENY, p. 81.
[19] FEENY, p. 80.
[20] FEENY, p. 83.

For don Leoncio, doña Rosita is the very incarnation of motherhood, so much so that he almost wants to worship her. Nevertheless, this maternal image is elsewhere described by don Cástulo as a «vieja-niña o niña-vieja» (IV, 388). Doña Rosita combines the wisdom of age and the innocence of the child: «Llevaba en el pecho una emoción deliciosa, pueril y senil» (IV, 339), and Conchona describes her as «—¡Santina de Dios! Con más años que el cuervo y más inocente que la paloma» (IV, 360).

Another dualism within the same person is *voluntad* versus *abulia*. Two characters in the novel, Paolo and don Cástulo, lead public lives of *abulia* and dream lives of *voluntad*. Paolo is another character who remains a child in the sense that he is completely dominated by his mother. Although he is nearly sixty, she has not yet allowed him to marry because she considers him too young. Paolo is incapable of confronting her, so he sublimates his frustration with physical activity and imaginary adventures. For this reason, he is attracted by his servant's tales of erotic escapades and by the drama of kidnapping Simona from the convent.

Don Cástulo also leads a double life:

> Era, sí, don Cástulo superlativamente candoroso en su corazón y conducta; no así en su imaginación. Don Cástulo vivía dos vidas paralelas, autónomas y sin mutuo contacto entre sí: una vida real y una vida imaginaria. Los ratos de ocio y solaz los consumía en leer autores eróticos, griegos y latinos. Su imaginación estaba atiborrada de erotismo literario y vaporoso, que jamás se insertaba en la vida real, por falta de datos de los sentidos y puntos de referencia experimentales. (IV, 247)

He is aware of this discrepancy and makes fun of himself: «Y eso que yo nunca sueño dormido, porque me acuesto cansado, entre otras cosas, de soñar despierto» (IV, 297). His name is also significant—Cástulo Colera; *casto* he is in action but not in thought, and the last name is ironic, given his timidity.

The one who is able to integrate the opposition between *voluntad* and *abulia* is Urbano, the prototype of masculine unification. Shortly after his marriage, Urbano has the same experience that Alberto had in front of the mirror—he is unhappily aware of the lack of unity within himself. But as his love for Simona grows, Urbano becomes a new man:

> Es que, de pronto, habían aflorado en la zona clara de su conciencia unas pocas palabras aprendidas muchos, muchos años antes, siendo niño, cuando cursaba Psicología. «Espinoza define el alma: *idea sui corporis* (la idea de su cuerpo).» La idea del cuerpo, ¿de quién? Ahora, aquella en otro tiempo indescifrable definición se alumbraba de un resplandor nítido. La noche anterior, Urbano había adquirido la idea del cuerpo de Simona; es decir, había adquirido un alma. Hasta entonces, había sido un hombre inanimado; ahora era un hombre completo, con las prerrogativas de la intimidad y la noción de la conducta; hombre interior y hombre activo; alma y cuerpo. (IV, 330-31)

He differs greatly from the protagonist of the tetralogy. Alberto, an *abúlico*, fails to integrate his personality, whereas Urbano has great strength of will (in him there is a great deal of the Nietzchean superman), and he shows that the man of action and the man of thought are not necessarily incompatible:

> Un día, al lado de Simona..., Urbano, como esos extraordinarios frutos mellizos que nacen y crecen dentro de una misma piel, se había contemplado escindido en dos hombres, sin detrimento de la unidad de su persona: uno, el hombre externo, activo y práctico; otro, el hombre espiritual, discursivo y analítico. Ambos hombres habían hallado ahora ocupación incesante. (IV, 469-70)

It is awareness of and union with his complementary opposite that help Urbano achieve a complete integration of personality. Alberto is never able to be united with Fina. As he walks along the trolley tracks, he sees his life running parallel to hers but never able to meet. «'Estoy perdido', se dijo» (I, 317) and, in fact, he is. In the tetralogy, the dualistic opposites are never able to be joined, a fact which seems to explain the melancholy and pessimism of those novels. But in the more mature works, Ayala moves continuously toward the unification of opposites and integration of personality. Within the same person, then, we find the dualistic opposites of masculine and feminine, parent and child, idealism and action, all occurring together in constantly shifting patterns, and all important in forming the complete man: «El alma humana está integrada de contrarios en equilibrio inestable» (IV, 232).

IDEALISM VERSUS REALISM

César Barja considers the basic conflict in this novel to be between the spiritual and the material worlds. [21] This opposition between the ideal and the real is shown particularly with regard to love.

Urbano receives a great shock when he finds out about the reality of procreation as contrasted to his idealized concept of love. He considers it unjust of God to mislead men into believing they are in love when it is nothing more than the instinct for the preservation of the species. Don Leoncio tries to explain to him the difference between «Amor» and «amor»:

> ¿Qué es el amor?, preguntamos ilusionados. Nadie nos lo quiere decir. El amor, nos responden evasivamente, es el Amor, todo el mundo lo sabe. Entonces, un día, llegamos también a saber lo que es el amor. Pero lo tenemos que aprender de tapadillo, cuchicheando. ... El Amor palabra, palabra vacía, es lo óptimo. El amor acto, el amor encarnado, es lo pésimo. La Iglesia y la sociedad sólo toleran el acto de amor oculto, disfrazado de sacramento y contrato: el matrimonio. Únicamente así el amor es limpio y legítimo; de otra suerte, es pecado y delito. (IV, 455-56)

[21] BARJA, p. 444.

Here is a clear example of the kind of categorizing mentioned in the Introduction: concepts categorize and define, but life itself is not so clear-cut. Love as a concept and a definition becomes the ideal, and the human act of love, the real.

Leoncio tells Urbano that the Church and society will permit love only within the bounds of marriage; love outside marriage is considered a sin. But Pérez de Ayala seems to advocate the acceptance of all love, with or without the disguise of sacrament or contract. When Simona tells the nun that, if Urbano wishes to divorce her and then have her as his mistress, she will naturally acquiesce, she disconcerts the nun because this perfect obedience has always been considered a virtue in the Christian wife:

> —Hija mía, no sé qué responderte. Si Dios ha hecho la mujer para compañera del hombre y que le ame con un amor ideal y perfecto, ese amor es el tuyo. A mí me han enseñado que amar fuera del matrimonio es pecado gravísimo. Pero si Dios te ha oído hace un instante, que sí te ha oído, pues todo lo oye, no sé por qué me imagino estar viéndole aprobarte con movimientos de cabeza, sonriendo paternalmente y agitando con dulzura sus anchas barbas de nieve. Y que Él me perdone si acabo de decir un magno desatino. (IV, 519)

There is also the contrast between love that is given freely and love that is bought. Urbano fears that Simona, who has been taken to a home for wayward girls, may learn more than he. He begins to study prostitution and—only as an observer—to visit brothels. His mother, in one of her invectives against wealth (when she became poor, Micaela suddenly turned against wealth), says:

> El primer hombre que acuñó una moneda introdujo la prostitución en el mundo. El dinero lo prostituye todo, hasta el amor, que por naturaleza no se puede comprar ni vender. Llamamos prostitución nada más que el amor corrompido por el dinero, porque es la peor de las infamias del oro. No nos causa tanta consternación y malestar esa palabra aplicada al poder, a la justicia, a la verdad, como aplicada al amor, porque nunca llegamos a convencernos de que el oro pueda prostituir al amor. (IV, 525)

What doña Micaela has noticed is that we are shocked when idealized love is brought down to the material (and materialistic) world.

There is a pícaro in this novel—Paolo's servant, *el Pentámetro*. In common with the tradition of such servants, he is thoroughly materialistic and, consequently, his view of love differs from that of doña Micaela. He also compares love and gold, but comes to a different conclusion:

> «¿Llave, el oro, que abre todas las puertas? —decía el *Pentámetro* con mueca ladina—. ¡Quiá! El amor. Para abrir puertas, la ganzúa. El amor es ganzúa. Más vale el amor que el oro. Con oro no se compra amor, si no es amor falsificado. Con amor se sonsacan y socaliñan cobre, plata y oro. Quiéranme las mujeres; nada me faltará...» (IV, 500)

The pícaro servant is also used as a contrast to the idealistic *señorito*. While Urbano is upstairs with Simona, the Pentámetro enjoys a good meal in the kitchen. Later, he tells Urbano: «Cada quisque busca en la feria lo que mejor le cuadre. Usté cenó suspiros; yo sopa de almendras, besugo y capón» (IV, 504). Thus we have in the novel the contrast between the ideal of love and its reality. Baquero Goyanes has pointed out that in the balcony scene, there are gradations of love from the pure and ethereal to the animalistic:

> Los amores —todo delicadeza— de Urbano y Simona en el balcón se ven enfrentados, en grotesco contrapunto, a los no tan delicados de don Cástulo y Conchona. El contraste de los dos idilios queda reforzado con «los maullidos escabrosos de dos gatos que se hacían el amor a su modo, con escándalo». La descripción equivale a una especie de gradación climática descendente, en que la tonalidad amorosa baja desde la eternidad del dúo Urbano-Simona en el balcón a la materialidad pingüe encarnada en Conchona y su don Cástulo, para caer en la desnuda animalidad de los amores gatunos. [22]

Aside from the main contrast between the ideal of love and its reality, there are other examples in the novel of the real versus ideal dualism:

Don Cástulo is reading Rousseau's *Émile*, a book which suggests that children should not be educated by books but rather by direct observation of nature. Urbano points out the discrepancy of a book's advising not to read books, whereupon don Cástulo answers:

> Sí, Urbano mío; los libros son mi vida, mi mundo, mi Naturaleza, y no podría vivir sin ellos... Pero, ¡por Dios!, no leas libros. Quiero decir, no leas libros todavía. Léelos luego, todos los que puedas, a tu tiempo; que colaboren en tus reflexiones sobre tu vida pasada, pero que no se antepongan a tus experiencias, provocándote la embriaguez de una vida imaginaria que te dejará inútil para la vida verdadera. (IV, 324)

Simona, traveling in the stagecoach on her first honeymoon, feels a «dardo centelleante en el pecho, que se le pasó de claro» and she takes it as a sign, like the one experienced by the Virgin Mary, that she will bear a child. She has no idea of the process involved in conception and childbirth; she knows only that married people have children and, now that she too is married, she is not surprised to learn that she will be a mother. However, by the end of the novel, when Urbano and Simona go on their real honeymoon, Simona is in fact pregnant: «Ahora estaba encinta, sin aparición del arcángel, ni tramoya celestial, ni nudo en la garganta. Estaba encinta como una mujer cualquiera...» (IV, 521), and she is able to tell Urbano that she is going to have «un hijo de mi carne; no, como antes, un hijo de mis sueños» (IV, 547).

[22] BAQUERO GOYANES, p. 191.

In like manner, as they travel in the stagecoach, Urbano daydreams about the possibility of being attacked and carried off by robbers so that he does not have to go with Simona on a honeymoon, the implications of which he does not understand and which make him uncomfortable. By contrast, on the second honeymoon, now fully cognizant of the meaning of marriage, his earlier fantasy comes true in that bandits actually attack the coach and he becomes a hero by fighting them off.

The polar opposition between the idealist Cástulo and the realist Conchona is apparent in the comical scene in which don Cástulo asks her parents for her hand in marriage. Don Cástulo first addresses the grandmother: «—Venerable anciana, bienquista de los dioses...» (IV, 438). Since the rest of the speech runs in that vein, the astonished members of the peasant family do not know how to answer because they have not understood a thing. Conchona has to translate: «Quier decise, hablando en cristiano, que el señorín cásase conmigo» (IV, 439). Later, when they open their school, don Cástulo wants to decorate all the classrooms with statues of nude Venuses, but Conchona is immediately aware of the consequences that this will bring: «o tener la academia llena de estatuas en pelota y sin un alumno o tenerla llena de alumnos y sin una estatua» (IV, 476). Don Cástulo sees the validity of her words but refuses to acquiesce completely: «Has dicho que sin una estatua; eso no. Una tendré en mi despacho: la de Afrodita de Melos... Prefiero no tener un solo alumno a vivir sin una sola convicción.»

MISCELLANEOUS OPPOSITES

The major dualistic oppositions that appear in *Las novelas de Urbano y Simona* are: two genres, two styles, and two myths in literature, nature versus culture, the male versus the female, dualisms within the same person, and the dualism of the ideal versus the real. There are of course minor dualisms as well, and it is significant that these, like the major ones, show a desire for integration.

1. For example, there are two contrasting ministers of justice who come to take possession of doña Rosita's farm. The kind one has a goiter, the heartless one has an unsightly skin disease. Oddly, the author himself confuses the two: A dialogue discloses that the man with the goiter is called Bartolo and the one with the skin disease is Celedonio (IV, 359). But two pages later, «Celedonio, acongojado, se llevó las manos al bocio, que era donde le dolía el corazón. Bartolo sonreía con insolencia» (IV, 361). While this may have been either an oversight or an intentional lapse on the part of the author, it serves to corroborate his idea that dualistic opposites are really interchangeable poles. The important thing is that,

from the point of view of Rosita and her family, the two men are interchangeable since both together bring the bad news.

2. Paolo is a lover of antiques. For him, however, antiques are not old but always fresh and young:

> El primer amor o debilidad de Paolo era su novia; pero de esto no hablaba sino veladamente. Sus otros amores eran las antigüedades, los libros de antaño y los caballos. Como quiera que su novia era vieja y sus caballos daba la casualidad que siempre eran viejos, Urbano pensaba que los amores de su amigo Paolo caían todos bajo el epígrafe de «antigüedades». Mas, para Paolo, las antigüedades jamás perdían su virtud juvenil, su frescura y sorpresa de cosas actuales. Su novia, en la frontera de la senectud, seguía para él, invariable, en la edad abrileña y recién púber. No variaba la novia, porque el corazón de Paolo era invariable. (IV, 506)

It is man, «el corazón de Paolo», who can unify and equate the contrasts.

3. Although not used as extensively as in *La caída de los Limones* the contrast between white and black appears several times. For example, they bury the grandmother in her white wedding dress and Simona consequently refuses to wear black at the funeral. The seven harpies who have custody of Simona own two cats, a Nordic white cat named Lohengrin and a Mediterranean black cat named Barrabas. The white cat is supposed to represent a blond man who will come to court one of the sisters; the black cat, a dark man. It is important that Urbano joins these two opposites: «'¿Cómo es tu marido?' —preguntaban a Simona—. '¿Rubio o moreno?' Simona respondía: 'Ni rubio ni moreno'. 'Será acebrado', comentaba Trifona...» (IV, 486).

4. Urbano also integrates the contrasts between the aristocratic art of fencing and the plebeian mode of self-defense, boxing. Paolo teaches Urbano fencing but refuses to have anything to do with boxing, a sport that Urbano has to learn from the Pentámetro. It is precisely because he is practised in both methods of fighting that Urbano is able to overcome the bandits that attack the stagecoach:

> Instintivamente pone en práctica las caballerescas destrezas de esgrima que le había enseñado Paolo y los ardides de pugilismo plebeyo que había aprendido del *Pentámetro*. Ya tiene a dos derrocados a sus pies. (IV, 545)

5. The polar opposition between truth and falsehood is analyzed and the conclusion reached that they each partake of the other, an idea repeated in *Tigre Juan*:

> Los cuentos de hadas son mitad verdad y mitad mentira. Lo triste de los cuentos de hadas encierra una verdad de la experiencia cotidiana, una verdad vulgar; la parte maravillosa todos sabemos que es mentira, pero es una mentira dulce, más preciosa y saludable y, en resolución, más verdadera que la misma verdad. (IV, 481)

6. In addition, the union between life and death appears in the figure of a cypress tree which has a rose bush «a él abrazado» (IV, 520). The cypress has long been associated with death for the apparent reason that the cypress, when cut down, does not put forth new shoots. This is true, of course, of other trees as well but, for some reason, the ancients gave this attribute only to the cypress. The rose, on the other hand, flourishes when it is trimmed; for this reason, it is a symbol of Paradise or eternal life. Again, it is important to observe that these dualistic opposites are embracing as if in marriage: «... bajo el ciprés desposado a la rosa...» (IV, 532).

7. The polaristic relationship between God and the devil is perceived by the astute Pentámetro. When he is planning how to get into the convent where Simona is being held, he decides that he must first seduce the doorkeeper: «La monja portera tendrá que ser. Con incienso me voy a perfumar, para hacerle cosquillas en la nariz. ¡Quita allá! Pazguato de mí. Olor a azufre, que no a incienso, la fascinará. Para una monja, ¿hay nada más seductor que el diablo?» (IV, 522). A few pages later, Urbano and the Pentámetro don hoods and masks to scale the convent walls and kidnap Simona. «—¿Quién eres, el amor o el diablo?—» asks the frightened nun. «—Los dos— le respondió una voz de profundis» (IV, 531).

Don Arcadio, the doctor who attends doña Rosita, is an old bachelor, set in his ways, for whom «la broma bufa era el matrimonio...» (IV, 369). Not so for Pérez de Ayala, who took marriage and its responsibilities very seriously. The main thesis of Las novelas de Urbano y Simona is precisely the question of how to prepare young people for a sacrament which holds as its highest ideal the physical and spiritual union of a man and a woman. The author seems to be of the opinion that, in order to achieve unity in marriage, the man and woman must first integrate their own personalities, often borrowing attributes from each other in order to do so. The next novel, however, presents a character who, on his own, becomes «nada menos que todo un hombre». Even though he marries and marriage brings fulfillment, he does not need a wife in order to integrate his personality. It is love, however, that starts him on the path.

6

TIGRE JUAN AND *EL CURANDERO DE SU HONRA*

Las novelas de Urbano y Simona dealt with two myths embedded in Western tradition, Adam and Eve and Daphnis and Chloe. These myths are parallel in that they both deal with the acquisition of sexual knowledge within a pastoral setting. The novels portray Urbano's gaining an understanding of his sexual nature and an acceptance of himself as a man and of Simona as a woman.

In the paired volumes that end Pérez de Ayala's career as a novelist, there are again two myths, but this time, they are peculiarly Spanish: Don Juan and, as Pérez de Ayala seems to have been the first to perceive, its corollary, the Calderonian concept of honor. The first book, *Tigre Juan,* explores the legend of Don Juan and the second, *El curandero de su honra,* is a parody of Calderon's play. Nevertheless, even though the titles show a major division, the themes of both books are actually interrelated.

Although the novel is based on myths, the «real» story deals with a character's quest for knowledge. This time it is not a quest for sexual knowledge, but rather a quest for knowledge of self, primarily in terms of how these two myths have shaped the Spanish psyche. The Tigre Juan story, like that of Urbano and Simona, works within two structural frameworks, one mythical and the other prosaic:

> The Realist saw the world, and this really meant society, as stable and subject to verifiable laws. ... At its most basic, Ayala's novel is not fundamentally different. Its central theme, marital infidelity, is common to many Realist novels. The theme, is viewed from a social standpoint, but at the same time it takes on layers of significance that transcend the merely social. The novel is composed of two worlds, one real, one mythical. ... On one level, the novel is a drama of recognition worked out through a web of personal relationships and specific social codes... The novel becomes a process of discovery. On another level, this process is represented in archetypal terms as a journey or quest. The social code is made known through its literary manifestations... as well as dealing

with a real and human dilemma. ... The real and the literary merge and their interaction is central in the final resolution of the novel.[1]

Pérez de Ayala, in his Tigre Juan novel, was able to integrate not only the real with the literary, but several other dualisms as well. Again for purposes of clarity, this chapter is divided into several subheadings: the fusion of dual themes in the Spanish literary tradition, the integration of the male and female dualism, patriarchal versus matriarchal values and their Freudian implications, the integration of the personality, and, finally, the dualistic musical composition of the novel.

The Fusion of Dual Themes in the Spanish Literary Tradition

The Don Juan theme became a popular literary preoccupation again at the beginning of this century. It was Pérez de Ayala, in a series of essays published in *Las máscaras* in 1917,[2] who first attempted a systematic analysis of Don Juan's character and the reason for his birth in Spain. For Pérez de Ayala, in his essays as well as his novel, Werther is the opposite of Don Juan. Werther represents

> the chivalrous and Christian attitude of the Middle Ages, the courtly love tradition, which places woman on a pedestal. Woman attracts by her beauty and man must prove himself worthy of her love. ... The cult of Beauty was centered on woman. In Ayala's view this is a predominantly Western outlook, Greco-Roman in origin, and against it stands Don Juan, whose cultural roots are Eastern and Semitic. The rigidity of the Jewish attitude to woman is reproduced in Islam and, because the Moors dominated Spain for centuries, the code of honour and its inevitable by-product, Don Juan, are characteristically Spanish.[3]

It was inevitable, therefore, that Don Juan be born in Spain. As for his personality, Pérez de Ayala has some startling insights. He says that Don Juan displaces the focus of love from the woman to the man:

> Don Juan viene a mudar los naturales términos de la mecánica del amor; el centro de gravitación y el fluido capcioso se oculta en él y de él dimana: Don Juan no ama, le aman. Y así resulta, curiosa paradoja, que el más varonil galán, galán de innumerables damas, pudiera asimismo decirse que es la dama indiferente de innumerables galanes, ya que ellas son quienes le buscan y siguen y se enamoran de él, que no él de ellas.[4]

[1] Macklin, *Pérez de Ayala: «Tigre Juan» and «El curandero de su honra»*, Critical Guides to Spanish Texts, 28 (London: Grant and Cutler Ltd., 1980), p. 21.
[2] Norma Urrutia, *De Troteras a Tigre Juan. Dos grandes temas de Ramón Pérez de Ayala* (Madrid: Insula, 1960), pp. 63-64.
[3] Macklin, *«Tigre Juan» and «El curandero de su honra»*, p. 26.
[4] *«Don Juan, buena persona»*, Las máscaras, Libro II, in *Obras completas*, vol. II, p. 343. All subsequent references to Pérez de Ayala's essays in *Las máscaras* will be taken from this volume.

This idea may have originated with Byron's *Don Juan*. It was further explored by Shaw in «Man and Superman», and by Otto Weininger. In his book *Sex and Character,* Weininger states that a woman is a purely sexual being and completely absorbed with procreation. Thus she will try to attract the man whom she considers most able to satisfy this need:

> A man demands chastity in himself and others, most of all from the being he loves; a woman wants the man with most experience and sensuality, not virtue. Woman has no comprehension of paragons. On the contrary, it is well known that a woman is most ready to fly to the arms of the man with the widest reputation for being a Don Juan. [5]

The irony is that, for Pérez de Ayala, Don Juan is not really virile. On the contrary, he has feminine qualities which bring out in women a masculine aggressiveness. [6] Thus, Don Juan is not the seducer; he is the seduced. In psychoanalytic terms, he is sexually immature, forever an adolescent. This is evident in his narcissism, his vanity, and his boasting. He is also a consummate actor, very talented in his art precisely because he is passionless. [7]

In this novel, the decadence and effeminacy of Don Juan is clearly shown in his physical description:

> Era guapo, con una belleza decadente de emperador romano o de señora madura en libertinajes. Despertaba en muchas mujeres atracción malsana y curiosidad de incertidumbre, no sólo por la ambigüedad de sus rasgos y miembros, algunos de ellos femeniles, como la sobarba, el abultado pecho y el trasero, no menos rotundo, sino también por sus actitudes sugestivas, de corrompida molicie, y su experimentada madurez... (IV, 679)

The name of this particular Don Juan, Vespasiano Cebón, is also significant. Vespasiano alludes to the decadence of the Roman emperors, and Cebón to a fattened pig. Since pigs are castrated in the spring to be fattened for a fall slaughter, the implication is that Vespasiano is impotent.

An important theme in this novel is «fama» and «lo que dirán». This is made clear in the very first page of *Tigre Juan,* where the author describes the houses around the «plaza del Mercado» as gossipy old ladies. The Spanish concept of honor has traditionally resided in «lo que dirán». Don Juan's reputation is also based on «fama». Vespasiano does not actually appear in the novel until the beginning of the second volume. Nevertheless, he is mentioned and talked about several times in the first

---

[5] OTTO WEININGER, *Sex and Character,* authorized translation from the sixth German edition (London: William Heinemann [1906]), p. 335.

[6] G. G. BROWN, p. 43, has pointed out the antecedent of an effeminate Don Juan in Clarín's *La Regenta.*

[7] It will be remembered that, for Pérez de Ayala, the actor does not feel emotions himself but, rather, studiedly provokes emotions in others.

part so that, when we do meet him, he is what we expect him to be. [8]
Thus, the two antithetical myths are related since they are both based
on «fama». In fact, the Calderonian husband, zealous about his honor,
would not exist without the Don Juan: «Although the two cultural heroes conflict, neither can exist without the other. The enemies are locked
together in complementary unity.» [9]

The protagonist of the novel is Juan Guerra Madrigal whom people
call «don Juan» out of politeness. Although he does not chase women,
he is a Don Juan in that he, like Vespasiano, can attract them:

> Pero jamás se supo de este don Juan trapicheo alguno, ni siquiera se le sor-
> prendió mirando a una mujer con ansia o insinuación. Sin embargo, a pesar
> de sus cuarenta y cinco años y de su temerosa y huraña catadura, o quizá
> por esto mismo, despertaba en no pocas mujeres una especie de curiosidad
> invencible, mezcla de simpatía y atracción; que es propio de la naturaleza fe-
> menina inclinarse hacia lo fuera de lo común y perecerse por lo temible o mis-
> terioso. (IV, 556)

Tigre Juan is no Vespasiano, neither in looks nor in reputation. On the
contrary, it is rumored that he had killed his wife: «Decíase que era viu-
do y había asesinado a su primera mujer; quiénes aseguraban que simplemente por hartazgo de matrimonio; otros, que como sanción de una
ofensa de honor conyugal» (IV, 557). Thus the two friends have opposing
reputations.

The intimate link between the Calderonian husband and Don Juan is
also made evident by the fact that, shortly before his wedding, Tigre
Juan plays don Gutierre in a local presentation of *El médico de su honra*. Vespasiano, having arrived in Pilares only that morning, uses every
histrionic technique in his possession to convince Herminia that the two
can be happy lovers after her wedding:

> A fin de asegurar el efecto, buscó una frase de conmiseración, lo que más
> lastimase el amor propio de Herminia, dejándola confusa, entregada sin al-
> bedrío:
> —¡Qué sabes tú, pobre provincianita!
> Después de una pausa calculada, prosiguió:
> —¿Que todo ha concluido? Si ahora empieza de veras... ¿Cuándo podía-
> mos, tú ni yo, soñar situación más favorable? Has cazado un marido que es
> un mirlo blanco: rico, en vísperas de viejo, chiflado por ti, que es como decir
> ciego juguete de tu voluntad, y, por si algo faltaba, mi mejor amigo en esta
> plaza. ¿Qué más hemos de pedir, vida mía? (IV, 680-81)

[8] There is a parallel here with Colás, who is the «caballero andante» of the novel.
Doña Iluminada feeds Carmina with tales of an idealized Colás, preparing her to see
in Colás her «príncipe azul». When Colás returns, Carmina has already fallen in love
with him.

[9] MONROE Z. HAFTER, «Galdós's Influence on Pérez de Ayala», *Galdós Studies, II*
(London: Tamesis Books Ltd., 1974), p. 25.

Vespasiano is conscious that he is acting as he plans to cuckold his best friend. That night, Tigre Juan is also an actor; his acting, however, becomes real:

> Tigre Juan vistió el don Gutierre de una manera que al presentarse provocó carcajadas. Como no disponía de mallas, se puso unos calzoncillos de franela color cresta de gallo. Colgado a la bandolera llevaba un espadón que le obligaba a dar traspiés. Se había pintado tenebrosamente entrecejo, ojeras y barba corrida, como facineroso. Pero después penetró de tal suerte en las situaciones del drama, era su ademán tan sobrio y convincente, su acento tan sincero, tan desgarrada y transida de llanto su voz, que el auditorio, sin advertir ya en pormenores risibles, se estremecía con un escalofrío patético... (IV, 683)

The fact is that Tigre Juan did indeed almost kill his first wife because he suspected her of adultery and, for him, Calderón's play is not illusion but reality.

This brings us to another dual theme in Spanish literature, illusion and reality. The reality is that Juan's first wife, Engracia, did not deceive him; he deceived himself, or rather, he allowed himself to be deceived by appearances and by his own fears. As Juan realizes in a moment of revelation, the man in Engracia's bedroom was not his wife's lover but the lover of his captain's wife. The Capitán had said, «Guerrita, hijo, en cosas de amor soy un lince» (IV, 624), a statement which Juan had found laughable because everyone but her husband knew of the infidelities of «la capitana Semprún». As a result, when he marries, Juan vows not to be as blind as the captain:

> Claro que, de casado, Juanín no se dejaría engañar tan burdamente como el papanatas del capitán. ¡Eso sí que no! Ojos de gato tenía, en la cara y en el entendimiento, que ni con la claridad del sol se deslumbran ni con la oscuridad de la noche se embotan. ... Adoraba a su esposa. Ella mostraba corresponderle con finezas tiernas y atenciones delicadas, que, por el instante, le aplanaban de felicidad. Felicidad amargada muy pronto por la pasión de los celos. (IV, 624-25) [10]

Because he is so concerned with being deceived, he ends up deceiving himself. The Bible says that «perfect love casteth out fear». If Tigre Juan had not been so fearful, he would not have been deceived. As the ghost of Engracia declares, «Te engañaste porque no supiste amarme bastante» (IV, 735). The answer, then, lies in love, which is equated with truth, as the only true reality:

---

[10] The symbolism of eyes, sight and blindness is recurrent in the novel: don Sincerato says that «los... ciegos son los que mejor ven, porque no han menester luz»; doña Iluminada has clairvoyance and Juan's maid is called «Güeya» which means «eye». Related to this symbol is the theme of light and darkness, especially in the person of doña Iluminada.

—No hay sino una gran verdad, así para el bien como para el mal, porque en ella se encierra la mayor dicha y la mayor desdicha.

—¡El amor! —afirmó Herminia...

—El amor es también un engaño —declaró Carmen, la del molino...

—De todas suertes, la dicha o la desdicha que este gran engaño ocasiona son las únicas verdades de la vida —dijo Colás. (IV, 735-36)

At the wedding of Tigre Juan and Herminia, a chorus of deaf-mutes had rendered a sign-language song which included the words, «La verdad es como el aire, / transparente y cristalina: / no la ve el hombre, mas siente / si le falta» (IV, 688). These words are later echoed by Colás, though he applies them to Herminia's new-found love for Tigre Juan. He again equates truth and love: «Estaba de Dios que Herminia hallase su amor cuando lo dio por perdido, porque el amor del cual vivimos, como del aire, no se siente sino a manera de privación, al echarlo de menos y asfixiarnos sin él» (IV, 742).

In the conversation between Colás and Carmen, there is a close relationship between truth and deceit, reality and illusion. They can become confused and, in some instances, illusion is preferable to reality and, indeed, can be more truthful than truth itself, as Herminia has discovered:

—Pues yo, a la verdad que me lastima, prefiero la mentira que me halaga, y con ella me abrazo, porque el gusto que la mentira me da no es mentira..., sino que es verdad, verdad, la única verdad amable. (IV, 661)

One of the most important innovations in the novel is the division of the narrative into two columns to indicate the separate but parallel lives of Tigre Juan and Herminia when they are apart: «La vida de Tigre Juan y la vida de Herminia, confundidas y disueltas en el remanso conyugal, se bifurcaron de pronto, como el río que, ante un obstáculo, se abre en dos brazos...» (IV, 709). In these parallel columns, the two dualistic themes of the Spanish literary tradition—Don Juan/honra and reality/illusion—are fused and integrated. Tigre Juan and Herminia discover a better concept of honor and love, and the truth and untruth of each. It is as if the two columns, one focusing on the myth of Don Juan (Herminia's) and the other on the problem of *honra* (Tigre Juan's), are the two pillars upon which the Spanish psyche rests:

The use of the double column... enables the honour theme and the myth of Don Juan to be worked out side by side. As Juan reflects on the multiple meanings of honour and reaches a new level of understanding which will form the basis of responsible conduct, Herminia is confronted for the first time with the true image of Vespasiano... The difference between Juan, the would-be Don Juan, and Vespasiano, the real Don Juan, is Juan's capacity for love, his ability and his need to establish a stable relationship with another person. ... As Herminia reaches this conclusion, Juan, in the other column, is beginning to realize just how problematic a concept honour is. [11]

[11] MACKLIN, «*Tigre Juan*» and «*El curandero de su honra*», p. 32.

In discovering that Don Juan, supposedly the epitome of the lover, is really incapable of loving, Herminia has moved from *engaño* to *desengaño*. Tigre Juan, on the other hand, because he realizes that love is the only truth, would now willingly accept the life-giving *engaño* of his wife's infidelity to a life of *desengaño* without her. Thus, whereas he previously prided himself on having the eyes of a cat, he now prays for blindness:

> —Señor y Dios mío: escucha mi ruego desde lo hondo de mi tribulación. ¡Que no se me pierda, Señor, que no se me pierda! Si has de llevármela por la muerte, sea antes yo burlado, con tal que ella viva. Y si para que ella y yo vivamos es condición tuya que me burle, ciégame, Señor, los ojos del alma y los del cuerpo, y así, no sabiendo ni viendo, viviré dichoso, aunque engañado. (IV, 712)

This idea is similar to the «mentira que me halaga» that Herminia previously defended. Moreover, Tigre Juan has learned a lesson from the devastating experience with his first wife and from the song of the deaf-mutes: «Lo que se oye no escuches. / No fíes de lo que miras»:

> Tigre no debería repetir el error que cometió en el pasado. Debería, en cambio, oír su propia voz interior: concepción del honor como «patrimonio del alma», no como sumisión a los dictados (injustos) de la sociedad... El hecho de que quienes ejecutan la canción sean sordomudos ejemplifica lo dicho. Se trata de un texto silencioso, sin palabras audibles. [12]

By using the polaristic literary theme of reality versus illusion, Pérez de Ayala destroys the other dualistic theme, Don Juan versus *honra*. The myth of Don Juan and the concept of *honra* are deeply imbedded in Spanish cultural tradition, but the author shows how false and erroneous they are.

The personality of Tigre Juan has made a half-circle. Whereas he previously defended Don Juan as the avenger of men and had acted the role of the Calderonian husband on stage and in life, he now puts his wife on a pedestal and is her willing and happy slave. He even goes on to imitate Werther, whom he had previously ridiculed, by attempting to kill himself for love. The transformation in Tigre Juan is exemplified by the fact that he considers it an honor to change his fierce nickname for a more pacific one: «—Llámenme, si quieren, Juan Cordero, y a mucha honra» (IV, 756).

In theories of love, the counterpart to Tigre Juan is his nephew, Colás, who started out as the *caballero andante*, worshiping his mistress from afar and going off to war in the vain hope of winning fame and fortune and her love. At the end of the novel, Colás stuns his uncle by becoming

---

12 CARLOS FEAL, «Don Juan y el honor en la obra de Pérez de Ayala», *Cuadernos hispanoamericanos*, Nos. 367-68 (January-February 1981), 95.

something of a Don Juan, advocating free love without responsibility or obligation:

> Colás... in the concluding episodes, now speaks deprecatingly of marriage and seeks a greater freedom in the love relationship. These views identify him more closely with the irresponsible Don Juan he scorned at the outset. Ayala's point in developing the characterizations through two novels is not to draw a change in his heroes so much as to affirm that the same person may embody opposing convictions. [13]

With regard to Don Juan, Tigre Juan has also come to agree with Colás. He has become aware that for his wife to be unfaithful, she needs a *burlador* and, as a result, she also is *burlada*. And he realizes that the concept of honor is based, in great part, on self-love and vanity: «... lo que sientes no tanto es amor a Herminia cuanto amor de ti mismo, amor propio y orgullo necio, pues te ha sacado de quicio el miedo a que opinen mal de ti» (IV, 714). [17]

True love gives freedom to the loved one, honor is self-imposed, and Don Juan is, in reality, «deficiente y castrado». These are the lessons Tigre Juan has learned. Because of them, he is able to forgive Vespasiano and recognize that his love for his friend is really a desire to be like him in some respects:

> Eres una parte de mí mismo, que me falta; como yo debiera ser una parte de ti. Te echo de menos; te echo de menos. Quisiera exprimirte como un limón e inyectar en mis venas porción de tu zumo ácido. Pero tal como eres, deficiente y castrado, te desprecio. (IV, 796) [15]

In contrast to a deficient Don Juan, Tigre Juan embodies true virility. He is «nada menos que todo un hombre».

THE INTEGRATION OF THE MALE AND FEMALE DUALISM

Tigre Juan is one of the few personages in the novels of Pérez de Ayala who does not at first show both male and female characteristics, although he later is willing to reveal some feminine qualities. The author

---

[13] HAFTER, p. 25.

[14] It is interesting that Pérez de Ayala, while reviewing a drama of Benavente, quotes a line from the play: «Sólo las mujeres son honradas. Los hombres no tienen honra. Lo que se llama la honra de los hombres no es sino vanidad» (III, 137). Our author seems to ridicule these words, but his own writings indicate that he agrees with them.

[15] Cf. WEININGER (p. 304): «People love in others the qualities they would like to have but do not actually have in any great degree...» Hafter (p. 27) has commented on the similarity of the ending of *El curandero de su honra* to the ending of Galdós's *Realidad*.

describes him as being completely manly. The dualism first evident in Tigre Juan is that of civilization versus nature in that from the waist up, he dresses like an *artesano* and from the waist down, like a *labriego de la región*. This duality is also exemplified by the contrast between his two best friends: Vespasiano typifies the urbane bourgeois merchant, whereas Nachín de Nacha is entirely rustic. Since, in most studies of dualism, civilization is considered masculine and nature feminine, Tigre Juan could be said to combine masculine and feminine qualities in his attire. His friends, on the other hand, exemplify the opposite of the traditional dualism; the civilized Vespasiano is the feminine counterpart of the masculine Nachín de Nacha. This is yet another example of how our author has fused previously dualistic elements and polarized them in this novel.

He also shows some dualities in temperament as, for example, his pride in being called «Tigre Juan»: «Es de presumir que le envanecía verse comparado nada menos que con un tigre, síntoma probable de no estar muy seguro de su fiereza» (IV, 556). The children of the town enjoy teasing him and pretend to run off in great fright when he jumps up with a scowl to give them chase, throwing handfuls of nuts after them. Then, for a while, he imprisons a couple of children in his keep, telling them he is going to fatten them up to eat. The fact that the children repeat this scene day after day, drawn by the nuts, shows that the children sense that Tigre Juan is not really as fierce as he pretends to be. Indeed, in spite of his nickname, his best friends «propalaban a todos los vientos que, en el fondo, era un bragazas» (IV, 556), and Colás, who knows him best, says: «Le conozco, su furor es repentino y pasajero. De león rugiente, en un punto se trueca en tórtola quejosa» (IV, 750). He has the reputation of being avaricious, yet no one can deny his generosity and tenderness toward Colás, an abandoned child he raised as his own. [16] In short, the odd combination of his last names, Guerra Madrigal, well sums up the ambiguities in his personality. In general, however, the townspeople view Tigre Juan as a completely masculine figure, and doña Iluminada considers him an «arquetipo de cualidades masculinas» (IV, 564).

The masculine archetype needs a feminine counterpart and doña Iluminada is satisfied that Herminia fills that role: «No te conocía bien. Me dejas admirada. No eres comoquiera. Eres toda una mujer» (IV, 661).

One of Pérez de Ayala's essays on the Don Juan theme, entitled «Weininger», describes some of the biological theories of this young, mad genius who lived in Vienna at the turn of the century and committed suicide at the age of twenty-three. He explains Weininger's ideas that all living

---

[16] FEENY has pointed out a hidden desire for paternity in Tigre Juan's relationship to the children, and his similarity to Belarmino in that they both lovingly raise children who are not their own.

things (plants, animals and humans) are composed of both male and female elements, and none is completely male or female. Sexual attraction is an attempt to reach completeness in masculinity and femininity. Thus, a man three-fourths male and one-fourth female will be attracted to, and attract, a woman who is three-fourths female and one-fourth male. Since Tigre Juan and Herminia are archetypes, they are each most nearly male and female. But even they are not completely so. Herminia responds with masculine aggressiveness to Vespasiano's femininity, to the point of chasing after him, and Tigre Juan, in his journey toward the inner self, will discover hidden feminine qualities. Nevertheless, since they are the most nearly complete in their masculinity and femininity, their union will form the archetypal marriage.

Just before her death, doña Rosita had lectured Simona about the wife's role in marriage:

> Abre el otro estuche... Es la pulsera con que me casé... Qué ancha es, qué pesada, qué firme; brazalete de esclava, porque la mujer pertenecerá siempre a su marido, y no habrá quien rompa esta esclavitud. Abre el estuche redondo... Acércate que te ponga esta diadema con que me casé, porque la mujer será soberana del marido y no habrá quien destruya este señorío. Abre esos estuches pequeños. Acércate que te ponga todos los anillos, como en una imagen de Nuestra Señora, porque la mujer será siempre una Virgen para su marido, no habrá quien enfríe esta adoración. (IV, 380)

As his betrothal gift, Tigre Juan buys Herminia a heavy bracelet on which are inscribed the words, «Soy de Tigre Juan». He gets so nervous as he tries to put it on her arm that everybody else has to help him, «de suerte que Herminia recibió la impresión de que no era sólo Tigre Juan, sino la sociedad entera, quien la esposaba» (IV, 673). Doña Iluminada echoes the words of Simona's grandmother when she says to the bride: «—Cerrada ya la pulsera sobre su brazo, Herminia, medita atenta lo que en este caso significa ese testimonio de esclavitud. No eres tú la esclava no, antes dueña y señora» (IV, 673). Thus society imposes on the woman a confusing double message. In either case, she is not given much choice.

Iluminada tells Tigre Juan that a good marriage is based on the free will of both parties, a thesis which Tigre Juan finds absurd: «Pues que Dios les negó mollera [a las mujeres] niégueseles voluntad y obedezcan. Soy con usté en que el matrimonio debe ser atadizo de amor para el hombre. En la mujer, obedecer es amar» (IV, 585-86). Later, however, he is made to realize that Herminia had indeed married against her will and that this was an injustice. It is only after she escapes that Herminia is willing to integrate the ambivalent role of slave and wife prepared for her by society. The difference is that she now chooses to submit to it. Weininger and Pérez de Ayala seem to agree that conjugal slavery is not a happy state for anyone; what the male really wants is a companion:

> But a great deal of what is taken for enmity to emancipation is due to the want of confidence in its possibility. Man does not really want woman as a slave: he is usually only too anxious for a companion. The education which the woman of the present day receives is not calculated to fit her for the battle against her real bondage... Women's education is directed solely to preparing them for their marriage, the happy state in which they are to find their crown. Such training would have little effect on man, but it serves to accentuate woman's womanishness, her dependence, and her servile condition. [17]

Weininger feels it is impossible to emancipate woman from her servility; the crown offered by marriage is only an illusion. Pérez de Ayala disagrees. This is evident in that Tigre Juan has changed positions from the Semitic attitude toward women as slaves to the European idealization of woman, which places her on a pedestal to be adored. The choice seems dualistic—slave or queen—but Tigre Juan has not abandoned one attitude for the other; he has amalgamated the two and each side will surface at different times. So Herminia ends up having both the master and the slave she dreamed of. In addition, by integrating the slave/queen dualism, Tigre Juan adds a third dimension to their relationship; he makes Herminia a companion. When the family is planning their vacation, Tigre Juan decides to take «la Güeya» so that «se ocupe a ratos de Mini y nos consienta algún vagar para juerguearnos tú y yo a solas» (IV, 763). [18] Seemingly, Pérez de Ayala was much more optimistic than Weininger and many of his contemporaries about the possibilities of forming a truly integrated marriage.

This archetypal marriage is symbolized by archetypal rituals during the feast of St. John. During this night, «los contrarios elementos, tierra y aire, fuego y agua, se penetraban y trasfundían en amoroso consorcio: la tierra se evaporaba y el aire se adensaba; el fuego se atemperaba y el agua hervía» (IV, 733). In this way, «the natural forces symbolize the depth of the passion existing in Juan and Herminia, link their experience to that of the whole universe and prefigure the union of the apparently irreconcilable». [19] What is important to note here is that the male/female dualism depicted as two parallel lines that could never meet in *La pata de la raposa* has been fused in *El curandero de su honra*.

Paradoxically, this union takes place while Herminia and Juan are separated. This «unity in disunity» [20] is shown by the two parallel columns that have promoted so much critical discussion. Carmen Bobes has said, «En cuanto a las dos columnas, es un fracaso del punto de vista semiológico porque no hay posibilidad de dar simultaneidad del tiempo real», [21]

---

[17] WEININGER, p. 348.
[18] FEAL, p. 102.
[19] MACKLIN, «Myth and Mimesis: The Artistic Integrity of Pérez de Ayala's *Tigre Juan* and *El curandero de su honra*», *Hispanic Review*, 48, No. 1 (1980), 30.
[20] MACKLIN, p. 30.
[21] Interview with Margaret Stock, Oviedo, 2 July 1983.

and Leon Livingstone has called the device a «brilliant failure» because «the reader cannot possibly absorb two columns at the same time and is thus forced to submit to chronological alternation in spite of the device». [22] Livingstone's article deals with the impossibility of representing the whole of reality within a linear narrative and suggests that Pérez de Ayala may have ceased writing novels because of a «feeling of frustration in the face of an insoluble problem». [23] Marguerite Rand mentions the possibility that Pérez de Ayala himself saw the difficulties in the two columns:

> It would seem that Pérez de Ayala came to the same conclusion, for, in the novel as it appears in his *Obras Selectas* (1957), there are no parallel columns. While their lives run parallel, the author narrates first the experiences of Tigre Juan and then those of Herminia. [24]

I believe that the division of the linear narrative into two columns is necessary. The author was well aware of the impossibility of simultaneous reading, for he warns his public:

> Ni Tigre Juan ni Herminia, a partir de aquel punto, podrían entender el sentido de su propia vida. Nadie pudiera tampoco, a no ser elevándose hasta una perspectiva ideal de la imaginación, desde donde contemplar a la par el curso paralelo de las dos vidas. (IV, 709)

The key word is «imaginación». The only way to comprehend the unity of the parallel columns is from the point of view of God, or of the artist, «pequeño dios», in other words, *sub specie aeterni*. The two columns are not meant to be completely parallel. No two lives are, not even in an archetypal marriage. However, as the two columns progress, the protagonists come closer and closer together.

> At first, if we read across them, we discover that a word or an idea bounces back and forth from one to the other, acquiring new shades of intent and disclosing inner antitheses; through this contrivance... the characters unwittingly engage in a dialogue. [25]

The culmination comes when the couple is reunited. For a brief period, the narrative is again divided into two columns, but this time, if only

[22] LEON LIVINGSTONE, «Interior Duplication and the Problem of Form in the Modern Spanish Novel», *Publications of the Modern Language Association of America*, 73, No. 4 (1958), 405.

[23] LIVINGSTONE, p. 404.

[24] MARGUERITE RAND, *Ramón Pérez de Ayala* (New York: Twayne Publishers, 1971), p. 120. Pérez de Ayala has used this device before. In *Luna de miel*, when the newlyweds are in the coach on their way to their honeymoon, the author devotes a few pages first to the thoughts of Urbano and then to the thoughts of Simona, broken up once in a while by the reality that joins them.

[25] WEBER, *The Literary Perspectivism of Ramón Pérez de Ayala*, p. 83.

because it is shorter, the unity is much more obvious. Whole lines are repeated in one and in the other:

> El momento clave de la novela se produce cuando Tigre Juan y Herminia vuelven a encontrarse...
> Otra vez y por muy breve espacio —solamente dos páginas— se abren las dos columnas, que, esta vez, sí son claramente paralelas: los dos piensan lo mismo y sienten de modo idéntico, desde perspectivas opuestas, así pues, es en este segundo caso —que no suele ser mencionado— cuando culmina la utilización artística del procedimiento de las dos columnas. [26]

In this scene, Tigre Juan and his wife are truly united in body and spirit. The author describes their eyes as fixing on each other in such a manner that it is almost painful to look away:

> Conforme avanzaban, Herminia y Tigre Juan iban volviendo la cabeza, que mantenían frente a frente, atados por la mirada, como si los ojos de entrambos se hallasen sujetos por una soldadura a los dos polos de un eje rígido. A cada paso que daban los portadores de Herminia, Tigre Juan, arrastrado, daba otro paso... Cuando depositaban a Herminia en el lecho, Tigre Juan ocupaba el umbral de la alcoba. En tanto iban las dos mujeres a desnudar a Herminia, Colás, al salir, tomó a Tigre Juan del brazo para apartarle de allí. No era que Tigre Juan se resistiese, sino que, aun queriendo retirarse, no se lo consentía la atadura de sus ojos a los ojos de Herminia; sujeción que al fin hubo de desgarrar con violencia, sintiéndolo, igual que Herminia, como una mutilación en carna viva, que a ella le hizo arrojar un grito y a él rugir por lo sordo. (IV, 745-46)

In *Belarmino y Apolonio,* the narrator had said that «el Aligator» and don Amaranto «estaban en la relación de los dos polos de un eje» (IV, 215), thus polarizing the dualistic concepts drama and philosophy. The love between Herminia and Tigre Juan presents the polarization of the male/female dualism, the most basic dualism of all. Another example of their unity is the fact that Herminia becomes increasingly nervous when Juan has shut himself up in his room to bleed himself. She repeatedly begs someone to go and check on him, and it is because of her insistence that they reach Juan in time to save his life. Her spiritual union with him had warned her of something wrong.

The symbol of their unity is the son they bear. (Tigre Juan burns himself on the calves in order to participate in the birth pains.) Juan, at the end of the narrative, sings a song to this union: «¡Hijo mío, que estás en mis brazos! / ¡Mujer mía, que estás a mi vera / y en mi tuétano estás impregnada, y estamos / alma y cuerpo, tú y yo, en este hijo de entrambos!» (IV, 769).

---

[26] AMORÓS, Introduction to *Tigre Juan y El curandero de su honra,* by Ramón Pérez de Ayala (Madrid: Clásicos Castalia, 1980), p. 55.

«El niño nació muy bello» (IV, 758), says the author. Quite a contrast to Prometeo. There are several reasons for this. First, the union of Tigre Juan and Herminia is a wholeness of masculinity and femininity. Theirs is a true, visceral love as opposed to the cerebral love of Marco Setiñano. This situation may reflect some of the ideas of Weininger:

> A second conclusion may be derived from heterostylism, especially with reference to the fact that «illegitimate fertilisation» [in plants] almost invariably produces less fertile offspring. This leads to the consideration that amongst other forms of life the strongest and healthiest offspring will result from unions in which there is the maximum of sexual suitability. As the old saying has it, «love-children» turn out to be the finest, strongest, and most vigorous of human beings. Those who are interested in the improvement of mankind must therefore... oppose the ordinary mercenary marriages of convenience. [27]

Tigre Juan married Herminia for love; Marco married Perpetua in order to father a superman. It was inevitable that Marco would produce a less fertile offspring. Another reason is that Marco cannot transcend his disappointment with the healing power of love. One suspects that Tigre Juan would have loved his son even if he had not been born beautiful. The description of the baby Colás, when he first fell into Tigre Juan's arms, is by no means flattering, yet the man felt an almost maternal tenderness toward the child. In his song, Tigre Juan praises God for his son's good health, but if he had to choose between goodness and life, he would prefer life: «¡Padre celestial! consérvamelo / sano de alma, / sano de cuerpo. / Mas si no ha de ser robusto, / como si no ha de ser bueno..., / ¡Dios mío!, consérvamelo» (IV, 770). This is the same kind of love he has discovered for Herminia, a love which demands nothing of the loved one except that he exist. Usually these feelings are associated with the mother, not the father. But Tigre Juan, like Belarmino, is not ashamed to be both mother and father to his child. He has successfully integrated maternal and paternal values.

PATRIARCHAL VERSUS MATRIARCHAL VALUES AND THEIR FREUDIAN IMPLICATIONS

In the Urbano and Simona novels, we studied how maternal/paternal attitudes, as well as parent/child traits, can all exist within the same person. The same characteristics appear within the personages of the Tigre Juan novels, although in a constant state of flux.

First of all, Tigre Juan is considerably older than Herminia, a fact which immediately implies a father-daughter relationship. The values he brings to the marriage are patriarchal in that man is the center of society.

---

[27] WEININGER, p. 43.

In that patriarchal society, the woman is subject to the man and has no being of her own except in relationship to him. Engracia, his first wife, had accepted this patriarchal code and defended his attempts to kill her:

> Proclamaba su inocencia, pero añadía que no podía probarla, porque tenía la lengua anudada por un juramento. Justificaba a Juanín y sostenía que, de haberla matado de veras, era su derecho y su deber, ya que las apariencias la condenaban... (IV, 628)

Herminia, however, is different and she upsets the patriarchal system by choosing to escape. Her flight is more an expression of free will than of love for Vespasiano, and for this reason it matters not if he abandons her:

> La postrera baza que tenía en la mano era el pecado. Como mujer, sabía, más por intuición inefable que a modo de conocimiento expreso, que si el orden de las cosas se suele disponer según leyes dictadas por el hombre, a las cuales la mujer está sujeta, en desquite en ella reside la suprema libertad de arbitrio, mediante el consentimiento en el pecado, puesto que, desde el Edén, el pecado femenino trastornó el humano destino y a cada instante desvía de su curso la vida de los hombres. Vespasiano estaba para llegar... (IV, 674)

In her maturation process, however, she becomes willing to accept the patriarchal system although—it must be emphasized—this is her choice. Perhaps it was what she saw of the lives of the prostitutes that made her appreciate her marriage. More likely it was the knowledge that she was going to be a mother and she wanted her child to carry his father's name. In either case, Herminia was confronted with the reality that her society was basically patriarchal and that there was no escaping its established system.

Just as Herminia becomes willing to accept a patriarchy in the person of her husband, so Tigre Juan also is able to recognize and accept another code of values that might be identified with a matriarchy. It is the clairvoyant widow who illuminates him:

> —Señora, vivimos en la sociedad.
> —Pero no para la sociedad. Tocante a ciertas ventajas que vivir en socie-dad nos proporciona, justo es que correspondamos sometiéndonos a lo que la sociedad, a cambio, pide de nosotros. Pero en lo atañadero a la felicidad del corazón, como quiera que de la sociedad nunca nos puede venir, no hay ra-zón para que consultemos a la sociedad de qué manera exige ella que nosotros hayamos de ser felices. Mientras no causemos daño a la sociedad, la sociedad no tiene por qué quejarse. (IV, 704) [28]

His love for Herminia and the joy that it brings him make him willing to give up his old patriarchal values of honor in favor of a more gentle tolerance, even in the face of ridicule.

---

[28] Doña Iluminada had previously said to Carmina: «—¡Ah, ya! La ley de los hombres. Pero hay, hija mía, otra ley, que es más santa: la ley de Dios. Y esa ley está en el corazón.» See also FEAL, p. 96.

Tigre Juan's conversion to a more tolerant social code occurs on the night of the feast of St John. On this night, he goes back to his archetypal Asturian roots. It is as if the trappings of civilization are slowly shed and he reverts to his most primitive self. The first description given of him mentioned that from the waist up, he dressed like an *artesano* or city dweller, and from the waist down, like a *labriego de la región*. The arrangement of clothing is significant. If the clothes of the city are on top, the implication is that they have been superimposed on his more visceral self, his sexual organs and his feet which touch the earth. These are his roots, as they are for all mankind. It is generally believed that the more primitive societies were matriarchal. Going back to his Asturian roots during a feast which may be Celtic or of more ancient origin seems to imply, therefore, a return to matriarchal values. The patriarchal values of his head and heart have been replaced by values which represent more truly his psychic origins.

There is also an implication here of a contrast between Castile and Asturias. Throughout his novels Pérez de Ayala frequently contrasts the two. The Calderonian code of honor would exemplify the Castilian, patriarchal system of values, as opposed to a more lenient Asturian acceptance of illegitimacy. Hence, the custom of *la covada* in Asturias, which, the author explains, was the way to establish paternity «con que la contada prole legítima se diferenciaba de la innumerable cría anónima, pues la mayor parte de los habitantes en aquella serranía eran hijos de madre soltera y padre desconocido» (IV, 757). It is also interesting to note that Pérez de Ayala's father was from Tierra de Campos, on the border between León and Castile (he considered himself Castilian) and his mother was Asturian. This would perhaps corroborate the association of Castile with the patriarch and Asturias with the matriarch.

Tigre Juan is reborn on St John's Eve. Symbolically, he becomes a child again and it is as a child that he now approaches Herminia. Carlos Feal has pointed out that this rebirth coincides in time to Herminia's realization that she is with child. The maternal in her is thus brought out, and her relationship to Tigre Juan can now take on mother-son characteristics. Previously, in the father-daughter relationship, the focus was on him; now she becomes the center of the new relationship:

> Así, pues, al hacerse Tigre Juan hijo, su personalidad se amplía. La «conversión» hay que verla en paralelismo con la experimentada por Herminia. Los dos integran en su personalidad aspectos contrarios a los hasta ahora vistos. De este modo se sientan las bases para una futura igualdad y, consiguientemente, una mejor, aceptable relación. [29]

Herminia compares her three suitors to skeins of yarn. The white yarn is Colás, a relationship in which she is the mistress and he the adoring

[29] FEAL, p. 99.

slave. The red yarn stands for Juan, the tyrant, and the need which she recognizes in herself to be dominated. Vespasiano is represented by the green yarn, a symbol of escape into a new and exciting world, away from the monotony of everyday life. The woman, therefore, feels the need to dominate (her husband would be her child), to be dominated (her husband would be her father), and to be excited (her husband would be a Don Juan). Her unconscious wish is to combine the three. With the conversion of Juan from *Tigre* to *Cordero,* she acquires the adoring lover in addition to the protective father. Her only remaining wish is for him to be a little more of a Don Juan so that she can have the excitement of being unsure of him. In the end, each has become parent and child to the other, as well as lover and companion. This situation has come about as a result of the amalgamation of their patriarchal and matriarchal values into one harmonious whole.

The Integration of the Personality

J. J. Macklin has made a convincing case for a Jungian interpretation of the Tigre Juan novels. He points out that Jung, like our author, had a «lifelong concern with the reconciliation of opposites...»[30] There is also an affinity with Jung in the use of archetypes and primitive rituals. For the purposes of this study, however, the aspects of Jungian psychology that interest us are the archetypes of the persona, the shadow, the anima, and the self.

The persona is the social mask that we wear. Some of the masks are obviously false, such as the persona of Vespasiano and of doña Mariquita, especially in the scene in which she comes to make amends to Tigre Juan for Herminia's rejection of Colás. Don Sincerato's face is described as an alternation between the «carátula de tragedia» and the «máscara de farsa» although, in him, these masks are not false. But the persona who interests us the most is Tigre Juan, mainly because his mask is easily penetrable (at least to the reader) and serves several different functions. He wears the mask of a civilized man in that he changes the way he speaks depending on whom he is addressing: «Tigre Juan atemperaba su lenguaje a la inteligencia, estado y estilo del interlocutor. Con las personas educadas procuraba hablar por lo retórico. Con Nachín de Nacha... empleaba voces y giros del dialecto popular» (IV, 559). With the children, Juan puts on the mask of an ogre although, instinctively, they feel his fundamental goodness and kindness. The adults are not so fortunate, as in the case of the dying Carmona to whom he tries to speak in playful jest, but whom he only succeeds in frightening: «Habíase esfor-

---

[30] MACKLIN, «Myth and Mimesis», p. 32.

zado ahora en componer una sonrisa benigna, melificada. A pesar suyo, presentaba una carátula de sayón, sicario o esbirro, que se refocilaba en el tormento de la víctima» (IV, 597). Paradoxically, the one mask he puts on consciously is actually the one that best reveals his inner self: «The biggest mask of all is Juan's 'persona' as the Calderonian husband: here the mask has a psychological origin as a defence mechanism.» [31]

This defense mechanism is a typical use of the persona to hide the shadow, i.e. the hidden, and usually repressed, set of negative or violent emotions that we cover with our persona and which frequently manifest themselves in unpleasant dreams. The shadow is most dangerous when it is unrecognized; the first step in the integration of the self is the recognition and acceptance of the shadow. Tigre Juan does not usually give free rein to his emotions with the result that, when they do come out, they explode. This is shown in his over-reaction to «la Güeya» on whom he has vented his anger upon hearing that Colás has joined the military. The crisis for Juan begins with the departure of Colás:

> Colás era pieza básica en el sistema de defensas de Tigre. Hacia Colás se volcaba la ternura del padre, que de este modo sin la presencia de la mujer, mantenía a raya la violencia de los afectos. Pero, al irse Colás, estalla la pasión; estallido que recuerda al de Tigre Juan asesino, y que así introduce la presencia de la mujer que quería borrarse. [32]

The letter from the Capitana brings the shadow out into the open. In quick succession, Juan weeps uncontrollably (in the presence of doña Iluminada), laughs hysterically (while playing cards that evening), and then faints from the shock of seeing Herminia for the first time. His reaction both to the letter and to the sight of Herminia is «¡La Apocalipsis!». The implication seems to be that, not only has the final judgment come upon him for his past sins, but also a new man will be born. The letter has made him remember detail by detail the story of his first marriage, and the sight of Herminia has reminded him so strikingly of Engracia that for him they are one and the same. The effect of all this is that his repressed shadow has been set free.

The rest of the novel will deal with Juan's reconciliation of his persona with his shadow, which, with the help of the anima, will lead to the integration of the self. However, Pérez de Ayala was particularly acute in not making this reconciliation a linear progression. Thus on his wedding night, even though Tigre Juan is well on his way to dealing with his shadow, it suddenly reappears to torment him in the shape of a prankster whom he mistakes for the lieutenant he had found in his first wife's bedroom. This incident also presents the Jungian idea that

[31] MACKLIN, «Tigre Juan» and «El curandero de su honra», p. 58.
[32] FEAL, p. 88.

the shadow is part of the collective unconscious and is therefore an archetype:

> De pronto, Tigre Juan se fijó, a pesar de la oscuridad, en uno de los fugitivos. Iba vestido de militar; llevaba bigotes a la borgoñona. Tigre Juan reconoció en él a un enemigo antiguo, muy antiguo; un enemigo que hubiese tenido en otra vida anterior. Era que aquel oficial, que ahora, igual que entonces, se mostraba tan diestro en la huida, se parecía, como una gota de agua a otra, al guapo y petulante teniente Rebolledo, el de Filipinas. De esto Tigre Juan no tuvo conciencia clara. Sólo veía en él un enemigo hereditario, como el gato en el perro, el cordero en el lobo, el judío en el cristiano y el burgués en el soldado. (IV, 690)

We have seen this recognition of the archetypal antagonist before, in *Belarmino· y Apolonio*: «... en el misterio del pecho eran íntimos el uno del otro desde hace muchos años» (IV, 211).

Tigre Juan's shadow has been set free primarily by his confrontation with the anima, which is, in part, a man's image of woman formed not only by his mother but by other women he has known. Thus, Tigre Juan's initial view of women is negative as a result of having observed the lack of sexual modesty in the girls of Traspeñas, a view which is later confirmed by the city women he meets, especially the Capitana. (Oddly enough, no mention is made of his own mother nor, for that matter, his father.) Thus, when Juan marries Engracia, he expects her to be unfaithful because all women, to him, have the souls of prostitutes. It is perhaps doña Iluminada who begins to change his attitude. She is the one woman, besides his mother and the Virgin Mary, whom he can respect. He believes she is faithful to her dead husband and considers her virginal in spirit. What he does not know is that she is physiologically a virgin as well. Her exemplary behavior is a revelation to him and prepares him for the change with regard to Herminia. When he sees Herminia for the first time, his first thought is that she is Engracia made flesh again. Later it does nót seem to matter whether or not it is the real Engracia.

> Quizás Herminia era retrato redivivo y reencarnación de Engracia. Quizás entre las dos no mediaba sino cierta analogía superficial de rasgos... Tal vez el lejano recuerdo de Engracia, recientemente reconstituido por Tigre Juan, no era ya imagen auténtica, sino más bien figura genérica en la cual pudiera coincidir e inscribirse cualquiera mujer joven, trigueña, agraciada y con ojos de oliva. ... Es lo probable, acaso lo inevitable, que en aquella disposición de su sensibilidad, fuese quien fuese la primera mujer joven y bonita que por ventura hubiera surgido ante él, Tigre Juan la habría confundido e identificado con Engracia. (IV, 637)

In keeping with the Jungian idea of the anima, Juan will simply transfer his anima to every woman who attracts his attention. Weininger would explain it again as an attraction of biologically complementary opposites: «Everyone possesses a definite, individual taste of his own with regard to the other sex... Every girl who strongly attracts a man recalls to him the other girls he has loved before». [33]

An important aspect of the anima is that, in addition to being a man's image of woman, it is also a representation of the feminine qualities in himself. The release of these qualities puts him in communion with nature and its beauties:

> Salió de madrugada al campo a recoger yerbas curativas. Todas las cosas le seducían; era llevado hacia ellas por un modo de amor nacido de la comprensión. Todo era hermoso. Todo era útil. Todo era bueno... ¡Qué linda, qué grácil aquella colina, con su contorno de seno femenino! Apetecía estrecharla contra el pecho como una esposa. (IV, 647-48)

This sudden reversal in Juan's feelings is perfectly in keeping with Jungian psychology:

> Jung conceived of the psyche as a play of opposites with psychic energy running, as it were, between two poles. These have a regulating function for when one extreme is reached the energy passes over to its opposite, a phenomenon known as enantiodromia in which, for example, anger suddenly gives way to calm, hatred to affection, and so on. This is what Jung designates the «self-regulating psyche»... [34]

The release of emotion is an important step in the path to self-integration:

> Woman teaches man, by fascinating him erotically, about emotion, about inner life. Thus the «anima» is also described as the link between the conscious and the unconscious... Love is a way of reconciling inner and outer, or integrating experience. [35]

The confrontation with the anima is the last step in the discovery of the self. By reconciling the persona with the shadow and by accepting the anima as part of the self, the ego can then begin to integrate these archetypal opposites. [36] At the end of the book, we see Tigre Juan perfectly content to reveal his anima when he feeds Mini and changes the baby's diapers. He does this completely unconcerned that the other passengers are laughing at him. His persona is no longer a mask but has been inte-

---

[33] WEININGER, p. 27.

[34] MACKLIN, «Tigre Juan» and «El curandero de su honra», p. 77.

[35] MACKLIN, «Myth and Mimesis», pp. 33-34.

[36] Herminia also goes through a Jungian process of integration. The fact that she has a «mancha carminosa» on the left side of her mouth allies her with Carmina (FEAL, p. 97). The position on the left side would suggest her «shadow», the hidden, rebellious side of her nature. Thus, when Carmina flees with Colás, Herminia becomes more than ever eager to flee herself. In the end, however, she has reconciled her opposites and wants to take responsibility for her own actions.

grated with the self. This sort of integration, according to Jung, «brings with it a feeling of unity with the whole of life, an acknowledgement of the existence of something beyond or greater than the individual».[37] Watts has explained this in mythological terms:

> There are myths of the creation of the world through the cutting up of some primordial being, of its division into heaven and earth, into the multiplicity of things, or into the two sexes... Thus many mythologies envisage the goal of life as the «rememberment» of this original «dismemberment». The human ideal becomes, then, the hermaphroditic or androgynous sage or «divine-man», whose consciousness transcends the opposites and who, therefore, knows himself to be one with the cosmos. [38]

THE DUALISTIC MUSICAL COMPOSITION OF THE NOVEL

The last page of the actual narrative shows Juan Tigre/Cordero breaking out in Dionysian song in an attempt to express his joy at being «one with the cosmos».

> Tigre Juan vela. Su conciencia se amplifica, se infiltra y diluye en las cosas, se confunde, con un escalofrío sagrado, en la conciencia cósmica. Piensa y siente por manera emotiva e inefable. Contagiado por el ritmo pertinaz y arbitrario del tren, también él siente y piensa con un ritmo arbitrario. [39] Sus pensamientos y sentimientos, cada vez más inefables, no se podrían traducir en palabras, a no ser aproximadamente. Y ya se sabe que cuando hablando del alma se dice aproximadamente, quiere decirse remotamente. (IV, 769)

Music may be the only way to describe the harmony of the universe. Perhaps that is why Pérez de Ayala chose to give his last set of novels their musical structure. *Tigre Juan* is divided into «Adagio» and «Presto»; *El curandero de su honra* contains a «Presto» and «Adagio», and also a «Coda» and a «Parergon». We observe a little of the sly humor of the author in that the parts seem to be paradoxically titled. The «Adagios» are full of dramatic action and intense emotion, whereas the «Prestos» narrate periods of relative calm. It should be noted that there is a duality of tempos; there are only two movements instead of three or four as might be expected. These dual tempos, however, are interchanged.

The Pythagorean concept which relates the harmony of music with the order of the universe is well known. Díaz-Plaja explains it as an attempt to create an ordered cosmos in the face of chaos:

---

[37] MACKLIN, *«Tigre Juan» and «El curandero de su honra»*, p. 88.
[38] WATTS, p. 46.
[39] Bearing in mind that Pérez de Ayala started out as a modernist, one finds that the following words from Octavio Paz's *Los hijos del limo* (p. 134) may be of interest: «El modernismo se inició como una búsqueda del ritmo verbal y culminó en una visión del universo como ritmo.»

Las mismas doctrinas pitagóricas exigen la doble consideración. Por un lado, la armonía surge de poner límites a lo ilimitado..., y la música, por ejemplo, es una sucesión del sonido (lo determinado) y el silencio (lo indeterminado). Es decir, que la música sería, por tanto, una síntesis de lo finito y lo infinito... [40]

Juan recognizes the terrifying chaos:

¿Adónde vamos? ¿De dónde venimos?
Medroso estruendo colma el silencio del universo;
el retumbo del torrente de la vida
en el vacío inmensurable
repercutiendo...
¡Padre! ¡Padre! Tengo miedo.
Tengo miedo.

(IV, 769-70)

In the end, however, the trinity of Heavenly Father (parent), Wife (companion), and Child help him find joy in life for its own sake: «Vivir. Vivir. Arrobo supremo», and he arrives at a classic solution: «El mundo es el sueño de Dios. / Sueño de amor. Sublime misterio». The novel ends with a happy Juan Guerra singing his madrigal to mother nature.

---

[40] DÍAZ-PLAJA, p. 204.

7

CONCLUSION

The two volumes dedicated to Tigre Juan ended Pérez de Ayala's career as a novelist. After that, he wrote mainly essays and some poetry. García Mercadal blames this silence on *abulia*. Amorós points out how busy Pérez de Ayala became with the advent of the Republic, his serving as its ambassador to the Court of St James, and then the subsequent exile in Argentina which was accompanied by pressing economic problems. Leon Livingstone has suggested that the author could no longer cope with the frustrating limitations of the prose narrative which, by its very nature, inhibits the presentation of the whole of reality.

I believe that Pérez de Ayala wrote his novels as a process of self-discovery. It seems significant that his last novel ends where his first novel took place: «El tren comienza a subir la dura rampa del Puerto de Pinares» (IV, 765). What a different scene we have here! Instead of a group of dissolute young men and women, we have a harmonious and loving family. The protagonist is no longer a pessimistic and unhappy youth, plagued with abulia as a result of an obsession with the irreconcilable dualities of the universe, but, instead, a fully integrated and mature man, who finds joy in the unity that he perceives both in himself and in the cosmos. Little by little, we have moved from dualism in the first novels, to a polarization of complementary opposites in *Belarmino y Apolonio* and, finally, to unification. In a conversation with Colás, Tigre Juan tried to explain the purpose of man's life: «¿Cuál es la razón de ser del hombre? Hacerse lo más hombre posible» (IV, 789). I should like to suggest that Pérez de Ayala, in his novelistic journey toward self-discovery, no longer felt the need to write because he had achieved this goal. In the previous chapter, I analyzed the process by which Tigre Juan was able to discover his inner self. Now I want to summarize the evolution that the novels show in Pérez de Ayala's own journey toward self-discovery.

The fact that Pérez de Ayala would see the world in dualistic terms was natural in view of his education by the Jesuits. Christianity is essentially dualistic and sees the world and humanity in terms of good and evil. This Catholic training was reinforced by a rigorous education in the Greek classics which also tended to divide things dualistically—reason and emotion, spirit and matter—especially after Socrates. In addition, Pérez de Ayala was well-read in the Spanish classics which favor the dualistic theme of reality versus illusion, as exemplified in two of its greatest works, *Don Quijote* and *La vida es sueño.* Considering his friendship with Einstein, I inferred a possible influence from modern physics and its relativistic view of reality. Einstein's vision of nature's inherent harmony parallels the tenets of the Eastern philosophies, and the polar union of opposites is particularly important in Tao. I also showed Pérez de Ayala's obvious preference for Spinoza over Descartes. Again, I would emphasize the relationship between Spinoza and Tao in that they are both monistic and see the Divine Principle not as a separate and fixed entity, but rather as a continuously moving force emanating from the universe itself. Thus it seems that Pérez de Ayala may have started out with a dualistic view of the world as a result of his early education, but that, as he matured and continued to read and think, he slowly changed from dualism to polarity and finally to a vision of the cosmos as an integrated unity.

In his tetralogy, Ayala makes much use of paired opposites: Cerda and Jiménez, Bertuco and Coste, Alberto and the *señoritos,* Rosina and the prostitutes, Alberto and Angelón Ríos, not to mention the titles of the chapters in *Troteras y danzaderas.* The use of paired opposites will continue throughout the novels of the author, but his interest in minor oppositions will decrease as his interest in thematic oppositions increases. So, in *Prometeo,* we have the opposing themes of Prometheus and Odysseus and of *voluntad* and *abulia;* in *Luz de domingo,* that of spiritual as opposed to materialistic values, and aristocrats against plebeians; and in *La caída de los Limones,* the contrast between a glorious past and a decadent present and the opposition between life/birth/light in contrast to death/night/darkness. The themes of major opposition in *Belarmino y Apolonio,* drama and philosophy, are united in the embrace of the two antagonists. Finally, in *Las novelas de Urbano y Simona* and in the Tigre Juan novels, we have the integration of the most basic dualism of all, male and female.

Although the author tends to use paired opposites in the tetralogy more than elsewhere, there is one major thematic dualism that he initiates in these novels and continues to develop in the others—the dualism of actor versus spectator. In *La pata de la raposa* Alberto feels alienated from himself as he looks in the mirror. He is conscious that he does not actively participate in or feel life but, rather, observes it from the detached position of a spectator. This opposition between feeling life and observing it is described in *Troteras y danzaderas* as «el espíritu lírico» and «el espíritu dramático», embodied in the paired opposites Verónica and Rosina.

When he reads *Othello* to Verónica, Alberto comes to the conclusion that the great tragedy is one which can make the spectator sympathize with the feelings of the actors to such an extent that it produces catharsis. However, there is no real attempt, even in *Troteras y danzaderas,* to fuse the spectator with the actor. We come closest to it in the scene with Verónica, but she can immediately sympathize with the feelings of each of the protagonists because she is an *espíritu lírico.* Rosina would not become so involved.

In *Tres novelas poemáticas,* Pérez de Ayala uses the poem-prefaces to serve as impassive spectators of the drama taking place in the prose narrative. The use of both poetry and prose implies that they are both necessary for a complete view of reality. This seems to be a first attempt at a binocular view that would integrate two ways of perceiving. The poem spectators synthesize and evaluate the actions and emotions of the protagonists in the drama.

Philosophy is also supposed to synthesize and evaluate and, in *Belarmino y Apolonio,* we have the opposition between the philosopher and the dramatist. Again the message is that they are both needed, one to understand and one to feel, but now the positions have become interchangeable. Thus, don Amaranto feels that the philosopher is the spectator *sub specie aeterni* and the actor in the drama feels the part he plays, whereas «el Estudiantón» is of the contrary opinion. The narrator says both opinions are correct. The dualism of actor versus spectator is intensified by the problem of language, which is also mentioned in *Belarmino y Apolonio*: as soon as a person starts to analyze and describe his actions and emotions, he becomes a spectator of himself. In this case, Belarmino would be the actor because he feels so intensely that he cannot speak, while Apolonio would be the spectator because his acting is a studied pose.

When Tigre Juan acts the part of don Gutierre in *El médico de su honra,* he is not detached but very emotionally involved in the role he is playing. He feels, and his audience intuits, that in acting out that role, he is portraying a real-life drama that he endured. But later he realizes that this was a false mask, not indicative of his true self, and he throws the actor's mask away. Vespasiano will always remain the spectator of his own consummate seductive act, but Tigre Juan no longer needs to be either actor or spectator. He has reached his true self and is unconcerned with how others view him or how he views himself. His only wish is to have a little of Vespasiano in him because he realizes that Vespasiano's role as Don Juan is attractive to women and he wants to be able to seduce his wife. Nevertheless, he knows that Vespasiano wears a mask and, for this reason, his final words to him are, «Te desprecio».

The dualism of actor/spectator is closely allied to that of *voluntad* and *abulia*. Alberto is aware that he prefers to observe life rather than commit himself to it and that is precisely why he is *abúlico*. His intellect, which is forever trying to understand, analyzes rather than synthesizes, and, as a result, he cannot act. The same is true of Teófilo Pajares, the poet, who is put in opposition to the life-force man, Fernando. The main theme of *Prometeo* is precisely the problem of *voluntad* and *abulia*. Marco had written to his uncle: «La felicidad está reservada al hombre de acción; pero el hombre de acción no inventa la acción: la realiza; la acción la concibe el hombre de pensamiento; luego el hombre de pensamiento debe preceder al hombre de acción...» (II, 610). But his uncle does not see such a distinction between «el hombre de pensamiento» and «el hombre de acción»; he feels that exceptional men reach the heavens only because others help them up. It is significant that it is in the transition period of the *novelas poemáticas* that the author attempts to show the need for both. As in the use of poetry and prose, Pérez de Ayala views the dualism of *voluntad* and *abulia* with binocular vision.

This dualism is not used in *Belarmino y Apolonio*. The two shoemakers are *abúlicos* in that they neglect their work and prefer to live in their imaginary world, but no blame is cast. Urbano, who starts out *abúlico* under the domination of his mother, ends up having *voluntad* as a result of his love for Simona and his desire to win her. We can see in this character that the dualism is no longer opposing but polaristic; one can be exchanged for the other, depending on the circumstances. In Tigre Juan, the dualism does not even appear. Tigre Juan has some education, but not enough to make him *abúlico*. On the other hand, he is not completely instinctual in that his decisions are based on studied reflection. Like the actor/spectator dualism, *voluntad* and *abulia* do not even exist for him because he has been able to integrate them so well.

Alberto had said that the knowledge of death causes *abulia* and that strong men and strong nations are like the cunning fox who will gnaw at its own paw to free itself from a trap, even though it may be left crippled. (Hence, the title of *La pata de la raposa*.) Arias on the other hand blamed his *abulia* on the impossible dreams that he conjured up in his mind and could not carry out in real life. This leads to another major dualism in the works of Ayala, reality versus illusion. The confrontation with the knowledge of his mortality makes Alberto lose all his ideals, but, since he cannot accept reality, he becomes abulic. Reality versus illusion is of particular importance in *Tres novelas poemáticas*. The author uses Spanish literary tradition (the epic, the *romance* and the fairy tale) to point up the ideal of past greatness in contrast to the sordidness of modern reality. The past versus the present are shown by the contrasts between the mythical Odysseus and the abulic Marco, between the noble hidalgos of yesteryear and the Becerriles of today, and in the greatness of Guadalfranco, when it was founded, as opposed to its decadence under the rule of the Limones. The language also reflects the contrast between the ideal and the real as Pérez de Ayala imitates the Homeric epic style in the poems of *Prometeo*, but parodies it in the prose by mixing erudite vocabulary with a thoroughly popular lexicon. The description of the two Limón sisters by the young law student shows this same mixture of language.

In *Belarmino y Apolonio* we witnessed the interchangeability of the ideal with the real in the scene between Pedro Lario and Juan Lirio on the Rúa Ruera. Pedro advocates a street in accordance with an ideal of harmony and usefulness as conceived by the Greeks, the founders of Western civilization. Juan is perfectly content with the incongruities of the Rúa Ruera as it stands, with all its hodgepodge ugliness. In fact, he finds its picturesqueness so attractive that he starts to sketch it, but, in the very act of doing so, he makes of the real street an idealized portrait, which Pedro Lario has to concede is beautiful: «—La calle no puede ser más fea. El dibujo no puede ser más hermoso» (IV, 41). The importance of this famous chapter on the Rúa Ruera is that binocular vision produces depth perception and consequent perspective, not only as a way to describe it, but also to bring together the dualism of the ideal with the real.

In the Urbano and Simona novels, the main problem with regard to the dualism of the ideal versus the real has to do with a spiritualized concept of love and its human manifestation, the sexual act. The humanizing of impossible ideals is shown by the fact that Urbano finally is able to love his wife both spiritually and physically, that she is carrying a real child instead of an imaginary one, and that his fantasy about robbers attacking the stagecoach comes true and he is able to cope with the situation.

In *Tigre Juan,* impossible ideals are also humanized. By mixing the dual Spanish literary themes of reality/illusion and Don Juan/*honra*, Pérez de Ayala destroys two of the favorite Spanish myths by exposing their falseness. Tigre Juan, in coming into contact with his inner self, with his basic humanity, rejects the ideals he had previously defended.

The most basic dualism of all is that of male and female, and here we again note an evolution in the novels. In *Tinieblas en las cumbres* we see man and woman as age-old antagonists in the struggle between Rosina and her employer, Barros. When she falls in love with Fernando, however, the antagonism disappears and she feels irresistibly joined to him. But Rosina and Fernando are separated and although they come together again in *Troteras y danzaderas,* she finds that Fernando no longer completely satisfies her. She has a need to be dominated by Fernando, but, at the same time, she enjoys the feelings of domination that she has with Teófilo. This is our indication of a woman's need to be both slave and queen to her man.

I have indicated that Fernando is representative of the life-force man. Alberto, on the other hand, is abulic and therefore he is never able to

consummate his love for Fina. He compares his life and Fina's to two parallel lines of trolley car tracks, always running along side by side but never
meeting. Because of his basic *abulia,* the cerebral Marco is also not able
to communicate fully with the more instinctual Perpetua, and the same is
true of Arias and Lola. So far, all the lovers have been unable to fulfill
their love and communicate with each other completely. The first sweet-
hearts that consummate their love both spiritually and physically are Cástor
and Balbina. But their love is described in such idealistic terms that it
becomes dehumanized, as though in an allegory. The love between Pedro
and Angustias, however, is the most human we have seen so far, but it
also is frustrated since they are separated.

It is not until the Urbano and Simona novels that we encounter a
conscious attempt to study and integrate the male/female dualism. The
whole novel is a view of the universe in terms of the masculine versus the
feminine: culture versus nature, Logos versus Pan, history versus *intrahistoria,* reality versus dreams, exterior versus interior, classicism versus romanticism. In the end, Urbano is able to consummate his love for his wife not
only by overcoming his *abulia* but also by acquiring some feminine percep-
tions that help him understand his own humanity and so develop from a
boy to a man.

The Tigre Juan volumes continue the study of the male/female dualism,
but in more archetypal terms. Here, the important thing is not the union
between man and woman but, instead, the integration in Juan himself of
the male and female aspects of his personality. The mixture of opposing
characteristics within one person has occurred throughout these novels. Thus
Fina seems to be cold on the outside but she really is passionate. Her sister
Leonor seems to be frivolous, but she is capable of great sacrifice. Meg is
a mixture of beauty and evil. Both Teófilo and Arias bemoan their contradictory natures composed of a good angel and a bad angel. People also
change, not only within themselves, but in relation to each other as well.
Thus, a husband can become either a son or a father to his wife, depending
on the circumstances, and a parent and child can also reverse roles, as do
Micaela and Urbano.

The integration of the male and female into one harmonious whole is
of primary importance in Tigre Juan. We noted the author's use of Weininger's idea that nobody is completely male or completely female, but that,
biologically, all humans are a mixture of both. Androgynous characters
appear throughout Pérez de Ayala's novels, starting with Nausikaá in
Prometeo and in the persons of doña Predestinación, Felicita, Novillo, the
Duchess of Somavia, the maternal Belarmino, Micaela, don Cástulo, Conchona, Urbano, and even Simona. Herminia is masculine in that she
pursues Vespasiano, while Tigre Juan is maternal in his love of children
and his adoption of Colás.

The male and female dualism includes other dualisms that we can follow throughout the novels, such as civilization and nature. In *Tinieblas en las cumbres,* corrupt civilization (Pilares) is pitted against idyllic nature (the second chapter which describes Rosina's background). The civilized and cosmopolitan Marco cannot come to terms with the natural Perpetua, but this difference is resolved in the union of Urbano and Simona. Finally, in Tigre Juan's attire, we can see civilization (the top half of his garments) and nature (the bottom half) integrated within one person.

A second dualism is a patriarchal Castile-León as opposed to a matriarchal Asturias. When Alberto surveys his surroundings from the top of the mountain in *Tinieblas,* noting that the lands to the south are arid and harsh in contrast to the voluptuous greenness of the north, Castile-León and Asturias are set in opposition. The contrast seems to be between the head (Castile) and the heart (Asturias), and it is resolved in the Tigre Juan novels by a definite option for the matriarchal Asturias as symbolized by the ancient rituals of St John's Eve. This is also related to the civilization/ nature dualism in that, by rejecting his patriarchal, «civilized» values and by coming into contact with his feminine anima, Tigre Juan is able to integrate himself with nature, which was what Alberto had always wanted but had been unable to accomplish. In a similar fashion, by Herminia's acceptance of the patriarchal values against which she had rebelled, she is able to accomplish the integration that had been impossible for Rosina; she becomes both slave and queen as well as companion to her husband.

In summary, the novels of Pérez de Ayala show a progressive harmonization of the following dualisms: paired opposites, actor and spectator, *voluntad* and *abulia,* ideal and real, past and present, the dualistic aspects of language, the male and the female which incorporate the dualisms of civilization and nature and of the central plateau and Asturias, and finally the integration within the same persons of contradictory characteristics. We noted that the first attempt at bringing together opposites appears in *La caída de los Limones,* symbolized by the equalizing circular dining table at which sit a republican and a priest, two aristocratic ladies and a lowly law student, and by the circle of morning, noon, and night, birth and death. In *Belarmino y Apolonio,* one of the unifying factors is language. Father Alesón imitates Belarmino's language in order to communicate with him. Belarmino buys a magpie in order to remember prosaic speech so as not lose touch with his daughter and Monsieur Colignon. Two telegrams bring about the embrace of the two formerly antagonistic cobblers. In his last novel, Tigre Juan changes his manner of speech in order to establish better communication with his interlocutor.

But the principal message in all the last novels is that the most important integrating factor is love. Fina and Perpetua know this instinctively, but Alberto and Marco are unable to overcome their rationalism and surrender to their emotions. In *Belarmino y Apolonio,* however, the message is

149

clear. When they are united under the laurel trees, Apolonio says, «—Pero, ¿no estamos soñando?... Apenas si toco la tierra en donde piso», and Belarmino responds, «—Parece un sueño. El tetraedro [el todo] es un sueño. Sólo es verdad el amor, el bien, la amistad» (IV, 212). For both Urbano and Tigre Juan, love is the factor that starts them on the path toward unity of spirit and body, not only with their wives but also with themselves. Such strong emotions as love and unity with the cosmos cannot be expressed with words. As a result, *Tigre Juan* ends with a song symbolizing the harmony of the whole universe:

> El mundo es el sueño de Dios.
> Sueño de amor. Sublime misterio.
> ¡Hijo mío, que estás en mis brazos!
> ¡Mujer mía, impregnada en mi tuétano!
> ¡Padre nuestro, que estás en los cielos!
>
> (IV, 770)

These are the last words of the actual narrative of *El curandero de su honra* and it seems to me significant that Pérez de Ayala wrote no more novels. The dualisms that had preoccupied him seem to have been resolved in a «sueño de amor» that is universal because it comes from God and has its earthly manifestation in the human trinity of husband, wife, and child. The changes apparent in his writings from the dualistic pessimism of the early tetralogy to the harmonious optimism of the later novels begin to appear in the *novelas poemáticas*, shortly after the author had married and had become a father. The process of self-discovery, started in the autobiographical *Tinieblas en las cumbres,* culminates in Tigre Juan's song. After that, Pérez de Ayala no longer felt the need to analyze himself. All analysis will henceforth appear in the objective form of the essay, while the subjective and synthetical will be expressed in poetry, perhaps because, like Tigre Juan, «su conciencia se amplifica, se infiltra y diluye en las cosas, se confunde, con un escalofrío sagrado, en la conciencia cósmica. Piensa y siente por manera emotiva e inefable... Sus pensamientos y sentimientos, cada vez más inefables, no se podrían traducir en palabras, a no ser aproximadamente» (IV, 769). Dualism is easy to perceive and analyze, and his early novels are replete with paired opposites; polarity is more difficult to separate and study, a fact which explains the meshing of themes and characters in his middle novels; but the integration with the cosmos, seen in Tigre Juan, is impossible to express in prosaic terms. That may be why Pérez de Ayala never wrote novels again.

SELECTED LIST OF WORKS CONSULTED

Primary Sources

Pérez de Ayala, Ramón: *A.M.D.G.* Edited by Andrés Amorós. Madrid, Ediciones Cátedra, 1983.
——: *Obras completas.* Edited by José García Mercadal. 4 vols. Madrid: Aguilar, 1963.

Secondary Sources

Agustín, Francisco: *Ramón Pérez de Ayala. Su vida y obras.* Madrid: Imprenta de G. Hernández y Galo Sáez, 1927.
Amorós, Andrés: *La novela intelectual de Ramón Pérez de Ayala.* Madrid: Editorial Gredos, 1972.
——: *Vida y literatura,* en «*Troteras y danzaderas*». Madrid: Editorial Castalia, 1973.
——: Introd. *Honeymoon, Bittermoon.* By Ramón Pérez de Ayala. Translated by Barry Eisenberg. Berkeley: University of California Press, 1972.
——: Introd. *Tigre Juan y El curandero de su honra.* By Ramón Pérez de Ayala. Madrid: Clásicos Castalia, 1980.
——: Introd. *Tinieblas en las cumbres.* By Ramón Pérez de Ayala. Madrid: Clásicos Castalia, 1971.
Baquero Goyanes, Mariano: *Perspectivismo y contraste. (De Cadalso a Pérez de Ayala.)* Madrid: Editorial Gredos, 1963.
Barja, César: *Libros y autores contemporáneos.* Madrid: Librería General de Victoriano Suárez, 1935.
Baumgarten, Murray and Berns, Gabriel: Introd. *Belarmino and Apolonio.* By Ramón Pérez de Ayala. Berkeley: University of California Press, 1971.
Bobes Naves, María del Carmen: «Ramón Pérez de Ayala, la obra.» In *Homenaje a Ramón Pérez de Ayala (1880-1980). Nueva Conciencia* (Mieres del Camino), Nos. 20-21 (October 1980), 17-36.
Brown, G. G.: *A Literary History of Spain. The Twentieth Century.* London: Ernest Benn Ltd., 1972.
Cejador y Frauca, Julio: *De la tierra.* Madrid: Jubera Hnos., 1914.
Clavería, Carlos: «Apostillas al lenguaje de Belarmino.» In *Cinco estudios de literatura española moderna.* Salamanca: Colegio Trilingüe de la Universidad, 1945, pp. 65-91.
Cvitanovic, Dinko: «Consideraciones sobre la mentalidad alegórica en *Luz de domingo*». In *Simposio Internacional Ramón Pérez de Ayala (1880-1980).* Edited by Pelayo H. Fernández. Gijón: Imprenta Flores, 1981, pp. 53-60.
Díaz-Plaja, Guillermo: *Modernismo frente a Noventa y Ocho.* Madrid: Espasa-Calpe, 1951.
Encyclopedia of Philosophy, 1967 ed. S.V. «Spinoza, Benedict (Baruch)», by Alasdair MacIntyre.
Feal, Carlos: «Don Juan y el honor en la obra de Pérez de Ayala.» *Cuadernos Hispanoamericanos,* Nos. 367-78 (Jan.-Feb. 1981), 81-104.
Feeny, Thomas: «Maternal-Paternal Attitudes in the Fiction of Ramón Pérez de Ayala.» *Hispanófila,* 62 (1978), 77-85.

FERNÁNDEZ, PELAYO H.: *Estudios sobre Ramón Pérez de Ayala*. Oviedo: Imprenta «La Cruz», 1978.

——: *Ideario etimológico de Ramón Pérez de Ayala*. Madrid: José Porrúa Turanzas, 1982.

——: «El prólogo en Belarmino y Apolonio.» *Boletín del Instituto de Estudios Asturianos* (Oviedo), No. 78 (1973), 141-55.

FRECHILLA DÍAZ, EMILIO: «Procedimientos narrativos en *Tinieblas en las cumbres.*» In *Homenaje a Ramón Pérez de Ayala*. Edited by María del Carmen Bobes Naves. Oviedo: Universidad de Oviedo, Servicio de Publicaciones, 1980, pp. 67-87.

GARCÍA MERCADAL, JOSÉ: Introd. *Obras completas*. Vol. I. By Ramón Pérez de Ayala. Madrid: Aguilar, 1963.

GUERLIN, HENRI: *L'Espagne moderne vue par ses écrivains*. Paris: Perrin et Cie., 1924.

HAFTER, MONROE Z.: «Galdós's Influence on Pérez de Ayala.» *Galdós Studies, II*. Edited by Robert J. Weber. London: Tamesis Books Ltd., 1974, pp. 13-28.

HAMILTON, EDITH: *Mythology*. New York: The New American Library, 1942.

JOHNSON, ERNEST A., Jr.: «Sobre 'Prometeo' de Pérez de Ayala.» *Insula*, Nos. 100-101 (April-May 1954), 13 and 15.

JUNCEDA AVELLO, ENRIQUE: «La mujer en la obra de Pérez de Ayala.» In *Pérez de Ayala visto en su centenario, 1880-1980*. Oviedo: Instituto de Estudios Asturianos, 1981, pp. 177-225.

LIVINGSTONE, LEON: «Interior Duplication and the Problem of Form in the Modern Spanish Novel.» *Publications of the Modern Language Association of America*, 73, No. 4 (Sept. 1958), 393-406.

——: «Lenguaje y silencio en *Belarmino y Apolonio.*» In *Simposio Internacional Ramón Pérez de Ayala (1880-1980)*. Edited by Pelayo H. Fernández. Gijón: Imprenta Flores, 1981, pp. 71-90.

——: «The Theme of the *Paradoxe sur le Comédien* in the Novels of Pérez de Ayala.» *Hispanic Review*, 22 (1954), 208-23.

MACKLIN, J. J.: «Myth and Mimesis: The Artistic Integrity of Pérez de Ayala's *Tigre Juan* and *El curandero de su honra.*» *Hispanic Review*, 48, No. 1 (1980), 15-36.

——: *Pérez de Ayala: «Tigre Juan» and «El curandero de su honra.»* Critical Guides to Spanish Texts, 28. London: Grant and Cutler Ltd., 1980.

——: «Romance and Realism: Pérez de Ayala's Urbano and Simona Novels.» *Neophilologus*, 64, No. 2 (April 1980), 208-26.

MATAS, JULIO: *Contra el honor. (Las novelas normativas de Ramón Pérez de Ayala.)* Madrid: Seminarios y Ediciones, 1974.

NEWBERRY, WILMA: «Ramón Pérez de Ayala's Concept of the *Doppelgänger* in *Belarmino y Apolonio.*» *Symposium*, 34 (1980), 56-67.

NÚÑEZ RAMOS, RAFAEL: «La unidad de *Belarmino y Apolonio.*» In *Homenaje a Ramón Pérez de Ayala*. Oviedo: Universidad de Oviedo, Servicio de Publicaciones, 1980, pp. 113-38.

ORTEGA Y GASSET, JOSÉ: *El tema de nuestro tiempo*. Madrid: Calpe, 1923.

PAZ, OCTAVIO: *Los hijos del limo. Del romanticismo a la vanguardia*. Barcelona: Editorial Seix Barral, 1974.

PÉREZ DE AYALA Y RICK, EDUARDO: «D. Ramón Pérez de Ayala visto por su hijo Eduardo.» In *Pérez de Ayala visto en su centenario, 1880-1980*. Oviedo: Instituto de Estudios Asturianos, 1981, pp. 139-50.

RAND, MARGUERITE: *Ramón Pérez de Ayala*. New York: Twayne Publishers, Inc., 1971.

RANGEL, VICENTE: «Las novelas poemáticas de Ramón Pérez de Ayala: una interpretación estilística de *Luz de domingo.*» *Explicación de Textos Literarios*, 7, ii (1978-79), 197-205.

READ, M. K.: «*Belarmino y Apolonio* and the modern linguistic tradition.» *Bulletin of Hispanic Studies*, 55 (1978), 329-35.

RODRÍGUEZ, ALFRED: «Algo más sobre los zapateros de Pérez de Ayala. In *Simposio Internacional Ramón Pérez de Ayala (1880-1980)*. Edited by Pelayo H. Fernández. Gijón: Imprenta Flores, 1981, pp. 91-97.

SUÁREZ SOLÍS, SARA: *Análisis de «Belarmino y Apolonio.»* Oviedo: Instituto de Estudios Asturianos, 1974.

SELECTED LIST OF WORKS CONSULTED

URRUTIA, NORMA: *De Troteras a Tigre Juan. Dos grandes temas de Ramón Pérez de Ayala.* Madrid: Insula, 1960.

WATTS, ALAN W.: *The Two Hands of God. The Myths of Polarity.* New York: George Braziller, 1963.

WEBER, FRANCES WYERS: *The Literary Perspectivism of Ramón Pérez de Ayala.* Chapel Hill: The University of North Carolina Press, 1966.

——: «Relativity and the Novel: Pérez de Ayala's *Belarmino y Apolonio.*» *Philological Quarterly,* 43 (1964), 253-71.

WEININGER, OTTO: *Sex and Character.* Authorized translation from the sixth German edition. London: William Heineman, [1906].